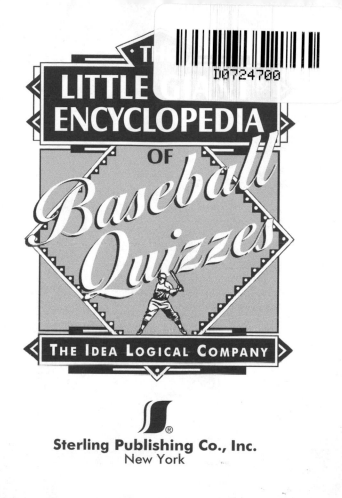

THE LITTLE GIANT ENCYCLOPEDIA

OF

Baseball Quizzes

THE IDEA LOGICAL COMPANY

Sterling Publishing Co., Inc.
New York

10   9   8   7   6   5   4   3

Published by Sterling Publishing Company, Inc.
387 Park Avenue South, New York, N.Y. 10016
© 1999 by The Idea Logical Company
Distributed in Canada by Sterling Publishing
% Canadian Manda Group, One Atlantic Avenue, Suite 105
Toronto, Ontario, Canada M6K 3E7
Distributed in Great Britain and Europe by Chris Lloyd
463 Ashley Road, Parkstone, Poole, Dorset, BH14 0AX, England
Distributed in Australia by Capricorn Link (Australia) Pty Ltd.
P.O. Box 6651, Baulkham Hills, Business Centre, NSW 2153,
Australia

Sterling ISBN 0-8069-1899-3

Contents

Introduction

In the 1980s, I led a team of about a hundred people that created 800,000 words of baseball history under 6,000 proper nouns that was published as a book, *The Ballplayers,* in the Spring of 1990. In 1993, *The Ballplayers* went out of print; if you can find one of the 35,000 copies publisher William Morrow manufactured, you'll probably pay more than twice the original retail price for it.

In 1995, Rick Wolf of *CBS Sportsline* (then called *Sportsline USA*), one of the two leading sports sites on the Web, discovered *The Ballplayers* and saw its potential as an online database. *CBS Sportsline* put *The Ballplayers,* along with the core of Jim Charlton's book, *The Baseball Chronology,* on its site in September 1997 as *The Baseball Online Library* where it remains, in a constantly evolving and updated form, available to baseball fans anywhere.

Meanwhile, my company, The Idea Logical Company, began providing other content to *CBS Sportsline,* which now includes two services graphically tracking the roster activity for Major League Baseball and NFL Football: *Baseball Fight for Jobs* and *Football Game Plan.*

And along the way, under our auspices, Stephen Holtje, who was the Managing Editor of *The Ballplayers,* started providing *CBS Sportsline* the questions each week for an online baseball trivia game. It is the best and most challenging of these multiple choice questions, along with an expanded group of possible answers, that provide the material for this book.

So what appears in this book is the work product of several people in The Idea Logical Company.

Stephen Holtje created the original questions and is the primary author of the material. James G. Robinson, the Editor-in-Chief of The Idea Logical Company, supervised the conversion of the online material into a book, replacing out-of-date questions, updating a few answers where what was correct had changed, adding the additional multiple choices, and double-checking research to confirm historical accuracy. In doing this, James was assisted by Idea Logical regulars Alexis Lyons, Michael Adler, and Noah Jurman.

Readers of this book who find this material challenging and fun can find a new set of questions each week at *CBS Sportsline* on the Web: (http://cbs.sportsline.com/u/baseball/bol/trivia/).

MIKE SHATZKIN
FOUNDER
THE IDEA LOGICAL COMPANY
http://www.idealog.com

The Quizzes

1. Who is the only pitcher in baseball history with two grand slams in one game?

1. Tony Cloninger
2. Dwight Gooden
3. Wes Ferrell
4. Babe Ruth

2. The major league record holder for most at-bats in a rookie season:

1. Nomar Garciaparra
2. Ron LeFlore
3. Dan Gladden
4. Rickey Henderson
5. Juan Samuel

3. Davey Johnson and Mike Ivie are tied for the ML record for most grand slams by a pinch hitter in a season with 2. Coincidentally, they accomplished this in the same season. What year?

1. 1976
2. 1977
3. 1978
4. 1979

4. Bobby Bonds hit a grand slam in his first major league game in 1968. The only other player to hit a grand slam in his first major league game is:

1. Ross Barnes (1876)
2. Bill Duggleby (1898)
3. Tony Lazzeri (1926)
4. Shane Spencer (1998)

5. Who is the only player with three consecutive major league seasons of 50 or more HR?

1. Cecil Fielder
2. Jimmie Foxx
3. Mark McGwire
4. Babe Ruth

6. How many pitchers have struck out more than 3,000 batters in their ML careers?

1. 5
2. 6
3. 8
4. 9
5. 10
6. 11

7. Who holds the career record for OF putouts in World Series play with 150?

1. Earle Combs
2. Joe DiMaggio
3. Mickey Mantle
4. Babe Ruth

8. John Smoltz and Tom Glavine are tied for the LCS record for most games started by a pitcher. How many games?

1. 8
2. 9
3. 10
4. 11
5. 12
6. 13

9. Wes Ferrell holds the ML season record for HR by a pitcher with how many HR?

   1. 7
   2. 8
   3. 9
   4. 10

10. In what year did the Seattle Mariners first finish a season with a winning record?

   1. 1989
   2. 1990
   3. 1991
   4. 1993
   5. 1994
   6. 1995

11. The record for most complete games pitched in LCS history is 5. By whom?

1. Steve Carlton
2. Ron Guidry
3. Orel Hershiser
4. Tommy John
5. Jim Palmer
6. Dave Stewart

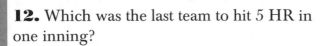

12. Which was the last team to hit 5 HR in one inning?

1. San Francisco Giants, 1961
2. Minnesota Twins, 1966
3. Boston Red Sox, 1979
4. Oakland A's, 1987
5. Minnesota Twins, 1987
6. Baltimore Orioles, 1995

13. What was the last major league season in which there were no no-hitters pitched?

1. 1978
2. 1981
3. 1985
4. 1989
5. 1991
6. 1994

14. Who is the only batter in All-Star Game history to reach base on catcher's interference?

1. Yogi Berra
2. Paul Molitor
3. Joe Morgan
4. Pete Rose
5. Willie Stargell
6. Mookie Wilson

15. Which pitcher surrendered Roger Maris's 1st HR in 1961?

1. Frank Baumann
2. Pete Burnside
3. Tom Cheney
4. Paul Foytack
5. Bill Monbouquette
6. Jim Perry

16. Who was the first person to broadcast a ML baseball game on the radio?

1. Harold Arlen
2. Tommy Cowan
3. Jack Graney
4. Harry Hartman
5. Sandy Hunt
6. Graham McNamee

17. Who was the last pitcher to reach 15 total 1–0 victories in a ML career?

1. Grover Alexander
2. Bert Blyleven
3. Steve Carlton
4. Dean Chance
5. Christy Mathewson
6. Nolan Ryan

★　◆　★　◆　★

18. Who was the last former Brooklyn Dodger to play in the majors?

1. Hank Aguirre
2. Bob Aspromonte
3. Don Drysdale
4. Don Elston
5. Wally Moon
6. Charley Neal

19. The first ML game in which both teams had uniform numbers was between the Yankees and Indians in what year?

1. 1927
2. 1929
3. 1930
4. 1931

20. Who was the last fielder to turn an unassisted triple play in the major leagues?

1. Ron Hansen
2. Davey Lopes
3. Mickey Morandini
4. Spike Owen
5. Lenny Randle
4. Ozzie Smith

21. When Rick Dempsey set the record for the latest inning for a 1–0 game-winning homer with a 22nd-inning clout, who was the losing pitcher?

1. Dennis Eckersley
2. Goose Gossage
3. Dennis Martinez
4. Lee Smith

22. Who is the only catcher in major league history to catch no-hitters on consecutive days?

1. Jim Hegan
2. Elston Howard
3. Hank Severeid
4. Birdie Tebbetts
5. Gus Triandos

23. Who is the only player to strike out in 12 consecutive at-bats?

1. Bobby Bonds
2. Bob Buhl
3. Rob Deer
4. Sandy Koufax

24. Who is the only pitcher to homer in four straight games?

1. Ken Brett
2. Don Drysdale
3. Orel Hershiser
4. Dave McNally
5. Don Newcombe
6. Red Ruffing

25. Zip Zabel holds the record for most innings by a relief pitcher in one game. How many innings did he pitch when he set that record on June 17, 1915?

1. 15.2
2. 17
3. 18.1
4. 20

26. Who is the only slugger to accumulate 500 home runs before turning 33?

1. Jimmie Foxx
2. Harmon Killebrew
3. Willie Mays
4. Mel Ott
5. Babe Ruth
6. Ted Williams

27. Who is the only pitcher to win consecutive MVP awards?

1. Carl Hubbell
2. Greg Maddux
3. Denny McLain
4. Hal Newhouser

28. Larry Jaster tied a major league record when he pitched five consecutive shutouts against the same team in 1966. Who did he victimize?

1. Cubs
2. Dodgers
3. Giants
4. Mets
5. Phillies
6. Pirates

29. Who is the only fielder to start two triple plays in the same game?

1. Gary Gaetti
2. Graig Nettles
3. Tony Perez
4. Ozzie Smith
5. Garry Templeton
6. Pie Traynor

30. Dick Radatz set the season strikeout mark for relievers in 1964 with how many K's?

1. 148
2. 155
3. 167
4. 174
5. 181
6. 189

31. Who holds the Los Angeles Dodgers' career record for games started by a pitcher with 533?

1. Don Drysdale
2. Orel Hershiser
3. Tommy John
4. Sandy Koufax
5. Jerry Reuss
6. Don Sutton

32. The Brooklyn Dodgers' career record for grand slams (13) is held by which slugger?

1. Roy Campanella
2. Babe Herman
3. Gil Hodges
4. Jackie Robinson
5. Duke Snider
6. Zack Wheat

33. Who holds the Mets team career record for most games lost with 137?

1. Roger Craig
2. Dwight Gooden
3. Jerry Koosman
4. Tom Seaver
5. Craig Swan
6. Anthony Young

34. The major league record for consecutive games driving in at least one run is 15 by

1. Steve Garvey
2. Ray Grimes
3. Mike Hargrove
4. Vada Pinson
5. Babe Ruth
6. Hack Wilson

35. Which Hall of Famer has the most career pinch-hits (77)?

1. Hank Aaron
2. Don Drysdale
3. Ernie Lombardi
4. Willie McCovey
5. Enos Slaughter
6. Duke Snider

36. Who holds the Cincinnati Reds' season record for slugging average (.642)?

1. Johnny Bench
2. Dolf Camilli
3. Eric Davis
4. George Foster
5. Ted Kluszewski
6. Ernie Lombardi

37. Who is the only player to play 500+ games at five positions?

   1. Harmon Killebrew
   2. Gil McDougald
   3. Jose Oquendo
   4. Pete Rose

38. Richie Ashburn tied the Phillies' single-season mark for fewest double plays grounded into two years in a row (1953 and '54). How many double plays did Ashburn ground into each year?

   1. 1
   2. 3
   3. 4
   4. 5
   5. 7

39. Lou Gehrig set the season record for most homers against one team with how many clouts against the Indians in 1936?

1. 9
2. 12
3. 14
4. 16

40. Who holds the major league record for runners left on base (12) in one game?

1. Jesse Barfield
2. Glenn Beckert
3. Hubie Brooks
4. Dave Kingman
5. Johnnie LeMaster
6. Danny Tartabull

41. In 1984, which Padres player set a team season record with 70 steals and another by being caught 21 times?

1. Tony Gwynn
2. Carmelo Martinez
3. Bip Roberts
4. Alan Wiggins

★　◆　★　◆　★

42. Who holds the Cubs' season record for saves?

1. Ted Abernathy
2. Rod Beck
3. Randy Myers
4. Phil Regan
5. Bruce Sutter
6. Mitch Williams

43. Who holds the season record for doubles (67)?

1. Hal McRae
2. Stan Musial
3. Paul Wancr
4. Earl Webb

44. Who holds the major league season record for fewest extra bases (9) when playing at least 150 games?

1. Rich Dauer
2. Bud Harrelson
3. Dal Maxvill
4. Mario Mendoza
5. Ray Oyler
6. Mike Tresh

45. Who holds the major league season strikeout record (189) as a batter?

1. Bobby Bonds
2. Rob Deer
3. Pete Incaviglia
4. Francisco Herrera

46. Who is the Toronto Blue Jays' career hits leader?

1. Roberto Alomar
2. George Bell
3. Joe Carter
4. Tony Fernandez
5. Lloyd Moseby
6. Willie Upshaw

47. What National League team holds the record for games lost over the entire history of the league?

1. Braves
2. Cubs
3. Dodgers
4. Giants
5. Phillies
6. Pirates

48. Who is the all-time total bases leader with 6,856?

1. Hank Aaron
2. Ty Cobb
3. Willie Mays
4. Stan Musial
5. Babe Ruth
6. Ted Williams

49. Who made the most errors (3) in one inning of a World Series game?

1. Hubie Brooks
2. Willie Davis
3. Butch Hobson
4. Fred Lindstrom
5. Sam Rice
6. Muddy Ruel

50. Who holds the American League career record for games played (3,308)?

1. Ty Cobb
2. Napoleon Lajoie
3. Cal Ripken
4. Brooks Robinson
5. Babe Ruth
6. Carl Yastrzemski

51. Who is the only pitcher to toss a nine-inning no-hitter in his first major league game?

1. Babe Adams
2. Bo Belinsky
3. Ewell Blackwell
4. Vida Blue
5. Bobo Holloman
6. Bumpus Jones

52. What pitcher has the most World Series wins (6) without a loss?

1. Whitey Ford
2. Bob Gibson
3. Lefty Gomez
4. Red Ruffing
5. Babe Ruth
6. Urban Shocker

53. Who holds the National League career batting record for bases on balls (1,799)?

1. Hank Aaron
2. Miller Huggins
3. Eddie Mathews
4. Joe Morgan
5. Mel Ott
6. Mike Schmidt

54. Who holds the National League record for most consecutive seasons playing at least 150 games?

1. Hank Aaron
2. Ernie Banks
3. Willie Mays
4. Pete Rose
5. Billy Williams
6. Maury Wills

55. Who holds the Pirates team career record for hits?

1. Barry Bonds
2. Roberto Clemente
3. Honus Wagner
4. Paul Waner

56. Who holds the Toronto Blue Jays team season record for hits (213)?

1. Roberto Alomar
2. George Bell
3. Tony Fernandez
4. Lloyd Moseby
5. Damaso Garcia
6. John Olerud

57. Who holds the Twins team season record for wins (25)?

1. Jim Kaat
2. Jack Morris
3. Jim Perry
4. Frank Viola

58. Who holds the Royals team career record for doubles (665)?

1. George Brett
2. Hal McRae
3. Kevin Seitzer
4. Lonnie Smith
5. Frank White
6. Willie Wilson

59. Who holds the San Francisco Giants team season record for batting average (.347)?

1. Will Clark
2. Bill Madlock
3. Willie Mays
4. Bill North

60. Who holds the Indians team season record for strikeouts as a batter (166)?

1. Albert Belle
2. Joe Carter
3. Larry Doby
4. Cory Snyder
5. Andre Thornton
6. Terry Turner

61. Who holds the Red Sox team career record for singles (2,262)?

1. Wade Boggs
2. Jackie Jensen
3. Ted Williams
4. Carl Yastrzemski

62. Who holds the Orioles team pitching record for longest winning streak (15 games)?

1. Mike Cuellar
2. Mike Flanagan
3. Dennis Martinez
4. Dave McNally
5. Jim Palmer
6. Steve Stone

63. Who holds the Browns team career record for games (1,647)?

1. Harlond Clift
2. Del Pratt
3. George Sisler
4. Ken Williams

64. Greg Vaughn set a Padres single-season record with 50 home runs in 1998. No Padre had ever hit more than 38. Whose record did Vaughn break?

1. Nate Colbert
2. Steve Garvey
3. Carmelo Martinez
4. Fred McGriff
5. Gene Tenace
6. Dave Winfield

65. Who holds the Astros team career record for grand slams (6)?

1. Bob Aspromonte
2. Jeff Bagwell
3. Cesar Cedeno
4. Lee May
5. Dickie Thon
6. Jim Wynn

66. Who holds the Expos team career record for games played (1,767)?

1. Warren Cromartie
2. Andre Dawson
3. Ron Fairly
4. Tim Raines
5. Rusty Staub
6. Tim Wallach

67. Who holds the Mariners team career record for stolen bases (290)?

1. Julio Cruz
2. Ken Griffey Jr.
3. Larry Milbourne
4. Craig Reynolds
5. Harold Reynolds
6. Bump Wills

68. Who holds the Atlanta Braves team season record for stolen bases (72)?

1. Brett Butler
2. Felix Millan
3. Dale Murphy
4. Otis Nixon
5. Jerry Royster
6. Claudell Washington

69. Who holds the Cubs team record for at-bats in a season (666)?

1. Cap Anson
2. Ernie Banks
3. Billy Herman
4. Rogers Hornsby
5. Jimmy Sheckard
6. Billy Williams

70. Who holds the Philadelphia A's team season record for home runs by a rookie (21)?

1. Frank "Home Run" Baker
2. Jimmie Foxx
3. Joe Hauser
4. Bob Johnson
5. Napoleon Lajoie
6. Al Simmons

71. Who holds the Rangers team season record for games won by a pitcher (25)?

1. Bert Blyleven
2. Kevin Brown
3. David Clyde
4. Charlie Hough
5. Ferguson Jenkins
6. Nolan Ryan

72. Who holds the Brooklyn Dodgers team career record for runs scored (1,317)?

1. Dolf Camilli
2. Jake Daubert
3. Carl Furillo
4. Babe Herman
5. Gil Hodges
6. Pee Wee Reese

73. Who was the first righthanded batter to hit 58 home runs in a single season?

1. Jimmie Foxx
2. Hank Greenberg
3. Mark McGwire
4. Hack Wilson

74. Who holds the National League season record for home runs by a switch-hitter (41)?

1. Bobby Bonilla
2. Ken Caminiti
3. Todd Hundley
4. Howard Johnson
5. Eddie Murray
6. Reggie Smith

75. Who holds the major league career record for home runs in extra innings (22)?

1. Barry Bonds
2. Roger Maris
3. Willie Mays
4. Babe Ruth

76. Who holds the major league career record for home runs as a pinch hitter (20)?

1. Gates Brown
2. Bernie Carbo
3. Cliff Johnson
4. Jerry Lynch
5. Manny Mota
6. Dave Philley

77. Who holds the major league mark for most home runs in opening games of a season (8)?

1. Eddie Mathews
2. Willie Mays
3. Frank Robinson
4. Carl Yastrzemski

★ ◆ ★ ◆ ★

78. Who led or tied for the league lead in home runs the most consecutive years (7)?

1. Jimmie Foxx
2. Ralph Kiner
3. Mickey Mantle
4. Mell Ott
5. Babe Ruth
4. Mike Schmidt

79. Who holds the A.L. season record for home runs by a second baseman (32)?

1. Joe Gordon
2. Bobby Grich
3. Rogers Hornsby
4. Davey Johnson

80. How many times did Babe Ruth hit 50 or more home runs in a season?

1. 2
2. 3
3. 4
4. 5
5. 6
6. 7

81. Who went the most at-bats in a major-league season without a home run (672)?

1. Mark Belanger
2. Rafael Belliard
3. Doc Cramer
4. Rabbit Maranville
5. Ray Oyler
6. Joe Sewell

82. Who hit 30 home runs in the most consecutive major league seasons (12)?

1. Hank Aaron
2. Jimmie Foxx
3. Ralph Kiner
4. Eddie Mathews
5. Babe Ruth
6. Mike Schmidt

83. Who was the first batter to hit four home runs in a major league game in consecutive at-bats?

1. Cap Anson
2. Ed Delahanty
3. Robert Ferguson
4. Lou Gehrig
5. Bobby Lowe
6. Pat Seerey

84. Who was the last pitcher to hit three home runs in a major league game?

1. Ken Brett
2. Don Drysdale
3. Guy Hecker
4. Red Ruffing
5. Sonny Siebert
6. Jim Tobin

85. Who was the last player to hit two home runs in his first major league game?

1. Bobby Bonds
2. Bert Campaneris
3. Bob Horner
4. Karl "Tuffy" Rhodes
5. Art Shamsky
6. Hoyt Wilhelm

86. Who was the first player to hit 30 home runs as a member of the Toronto Blue Jays?

1. Jesse Barfield
2. George Bell
3. Jose Canseco
4. Rico Carty
5. John Mayberry
6. Fred McGriff

87. Who was the first player to homer as a pinch-hitter in his first major league at-bat?

1. Brant Alyea
2. Gates Brown
3. Joe Keough
4. Les Layton
5. Eddie Morgan
6. Ace Parker

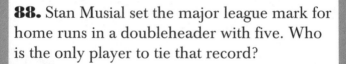

88. Stan Musial set the major league mark for home runs in a doubleheader with five. Who is the only player to tie that record?

1. Earl Averill
2. Nate Colbert
3. Jimmie Foxx
4. Roger Maris
5. Jim Tabor
6. Gus Zernial

52

89. Who holds the major league record for most three-homer games in a career (6)?

1. Joe Carter
2. Ralph Kiner
3. Dave Kingman
4. Don Mattingly
5. Johnny Mize
6. Willie Stargell

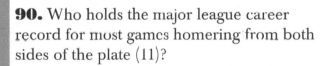

90. Who holds the major league career record for most games homering from both sides of the plate (11)?

1. Bobby Bonilla
2. Ken Caminiti
3. Todd Hundley
4. Howard Johnson
5. Mickey Mantle
6. Eddie Murray

91. Who holds the League Championship Series career mark for RBI as a pinch-hitter (3)?

1. Francisco Cabrera
2. Joe Girardi
3. John Lowenstein
4. J.C. Martin

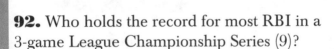

92. Who holds the record for most RBI in a 3-game League Championship Series (9)?

1. Hank Aaron
2. George Brett
3. Chris Chambliss
4. Reggie Jackson
5. Eddie Mathews
6. Graig Nettles

93. Who holds the League Championship Series career mark for bases on balls (23)?

1. Rickey Henderson
2. Reggie Jackson
3. Mark McGwire
4. Joe Morgan

94. Who was the first pinch-hitter to draw a walk with the bases loaded in a League Championship Series game?

1. Rod Carew
2. Duffy Dyer
3. Rod Gaspar
4. Cesar Geronimo
5. Mike Sharperson
6. Bernie Williams

95. Who was the first player in League Championship Series history with 6 at-bats in a nine-inning game?

1. Tommie Agee
2. Paul Blair
3. Rod Carew
4. Ralph Garr

96. Who has the most career triples in League Championship Series play (4)?

1. George Brett
2. Steve Garvey
3. Reggie Jackson
4. Bill Madlock
5. Mookie Wilson
6. Willie Wilson

97. Who has the most consecutive hits in a single League Championship Series (6)?

1. Paul Blair
2. Paul Molitor
3. Paul Popovich
4. Pete Rose

98. Who has the most League Championship Series pinch-running appearances (4)?

1. Lance Blankenship
2. Dave Concepcion
3. Eric Fox
4. Mike Gallego
5. Lonnie Smith
6. Dave Stapleton

99. Who was the first National League player to triple in League Championship Series action?

1. Hank Aaron
2. Tommie Aaron
3. Tommie Agee
4. Bud Harrelson
5. Art Shamsky

100. Who has the most career home runs in League Championship Series play (9)?

1. George Brett
2. Will Clark
3. Steve Garvey
4. Reggie Jackson
5. Darryl Strawberry
6. Todd Zeile

101. Who homered in the most separate League Championship Series (5)?

1. Johnny Bench
2. Dave Concepcion
3. Graig Nettles
4. Dave Parker
5. Joe Rudi
6. Gene Tenace

102. Who was the first player to score 4 runs in a League Championship Series game?

1. Will Clark
2. Steve Garvey
3. Reggie Jackson
4. Jay Johnstone
5. Bob Robertson
6. Brooks Robinson

103. Who has the most League Championship Series pinch-hitting appearances (10)?

1. Danny Heep
2. Dane Iorg
3. Lee Mazzilli
4. Manny Mota
5. Lonnie Smith
6. Rusty Staub

104. Who is the only American League player to homer in a 1–0 League Championship Series game?

1. Sal Bando
2. Don Buford
3. Dan Ford
4. Harmon Killebrew
5. John Lowenstein
6. Mike Pagliarulo

105. Who was the first president to attend a World Series game during his term of office?

1. Calvin Coolidge
2. Dwight Eisenhower
3. Herbert Hoover
4. Franklin Roosevelt
5. Woodrow Wilson

106. New York has hosted more World Series games than any other city. Which metropolis has hosted the second-most?

1. Boston
2. Chicago
3. Detroit
4. Philadelphia
5. Pittsburgh
6. St. Louis

107. Who has the most consecutive hitless at-bats in League Championship Series (31)?

1. Bobby Bonds
2. Bobby Bonilla
3. Bert Campaneris
4. Cesar Geronimo
5. Billy North
6. Terry Pendleton

108. Who holds the National League career record for extra-base hits in League Championship Series play (12)?

1. Will Clark
2. Steve Garvey
3. Keith Hernandez
4. Javier Lopez
5. Gary Matthews
6. Willie Stargell

109. Who holds the World Series career record for putouts by an outfielder (150)?

1. Hank Bauer
2. Joe DiMaggio
3. Mickey Mantle
4. Willie Mays

110. Who holds the record for most RBI as a pinch-hitter in a single World Series (6)?

1. Bernie Carbo
2. Chuck Essegian
3. Tommy Henrich
4. Cookie Lavagetto
5. Manny Mota
6. Dusty Rhodes

111. Who is the only player to play in 30 consecutive World Series games?

1. Yogi Berra
2. Gil Hodges
3. Mickey Mantle
4. Bobby Richardson

112. Who made the most career World Series appearances as a pinch-runner (9)?

1. Dan Gladden
2. Mark Lemke
3. Allan Lewis
4. Jose Oquendo
5. Lonnie Smith
6. Herb Washington

113. Who holds the career World Series record for games won as a manager (37)?

1. Walter Alston
2. Joe McCarthy
3. John McGraw
4. Casey Stengel

114. Who holds the career World Series record for games lost as a manager (28)?

1. Bobby Cox
2. Hughey Jennings
3. Connie Mack
4. John McGraw
5. Casey Stengel
6. Earl Weaver

115. Who pitched the most games in a single World Series (7)?

1. Darold Knowles
2. Mike Marshall
3. Christy Mathewson
4. Dan Quisenberry

116. Who holds the World Series career record for total bases (123)?

1. Yogi Berra
2. Joe DiMaggio
3. Reggie Jackson
4. Mickey Mantle
5. Joe Morgan
6. Babe Ruth

117. Who has the highest career batting average (.391) in World Series play in 20 or more games?

1. Lou Brock
2. Billy Martin
3. Pee Wee Reese
4. Bobby Richardson

118. Who is the only player to hit .300 in six separate World Series?

1. Yogi Berra
2. Eddie Collins
3. Lou Gehrig
4. Graig Nettles
5. Joe Rudi
6. Babe Ruth

119. Who holds the World Series record for most at-bats (7) in a single game?

1. Paul Blair
2. Rod Carew
3. Don Hahn
4. Rickey Henderson
5. Mookie Wilson
6. Willie Wilson

120. Who was the first player to score 4 runs in one World Series game?

1. Ty Cobb
2. Eddie Collins
3. Earle Combs
4. Frankie Frisch
5. Babe Ruth
6. Ross Youngs

121. Who was the last pitcher to start consecutive games in a World Series?

1. Jack Coombs
2. George Earnshaw
3. Whitey Ford
4. Christy Mathewson
5. Joe McGinnity
6. Deacon Phillippe

122. Who holds the career record for most chances accepted by a third baseman in World Series play (96)?

1. Ron Cey
2. Billy Cox
3. Graig Nettles
4. Terry Pendleton
5. Brooks Robinson
6. Mike Schmidt

123. Who was the oldest player ever to appear in a World Series?

1. Jim Kaat
2. Dolph Luque
3. Willie Mays
4. Joe Niekro
5. Jack Quinn
6. Pete Rose

124. What pitcher won the most opening games (5) in World Series history?

1. Jack Coombs
2. Whitey Ford
3. Lefty Gomez
4. Lefty Grove
5. Allie Reynolds
6. Red Ruffing
7. Joe Wood

125. Who is the only player to have 5 hits in a World Series game?

   1. Yogi Berra
   2. Bob Cerv
   3. Carl Furillo
   4. Paul Molitor
   5. Willie Wilson

★ ◆ ★ ◆ ★

126. Who struck out the most times (12) in a single World Series?

   1. Wayne Garrett
   2. George Kelly
   3. Carmelo Martinez
   4. Mickey Mantle
   5. Eddie Mathews
   6. Bob Meusel
   7. Willie Wilson

127. Who holds the career World Series mark for most times caught stealing (9)?

1. Lou Brock
2. Rickey Henderson
3. Otis Nixon
4. Frank Schulte

128. What team holds the record for highest batting average in a World Series (.338)?

1. Yankees, 1927
2. Yankees, 1939
3. Yankees, 1960
4. Yankees, 1978
5. Yankees, 1981
6. Yankees, 1998

129. Who pitched the most innings in a single World Series game (14)?

1. Walter Johnson
2. Christy Mathewson
3. Babe Ruth
4. Hippo Vaughn

130. Who is the youngest pitcher to win a complete-game shutout in the World Series?

1. Babe Adams
2. Steve Avery
3. Dwight Gooden
4. Jim Palmer
5. Babe Ruth
6. Bret Saberhagen

131. Which pitcher holds the career record for World Series losses (8)?

1. Whitey Ford
2. Walter Johnson
3. Charlie Leibrandt
4. Eddie Plank

132. Who holds the World Series career record for putouts by a second baseman (104)?

1. Eddie Collins
2. Frankie Frisch
3. Rogers Hornsby
4. Davey Johnson
5. Billy Martin
6. Joe Morgan

133. Who is the only pitcher in World Series history to twice retire the side in an inning on just three pitched balls?

1. Tiny Bonham
2. Whitey Ford
3. Christy Mathewson
4. Deacon Phillippe

★ ◆ ★ ◆ ★

134. Who holds the record for most double plays turned by a second baseman in a World Series (9)?

1. Carlos Baerga
2. Jerry Coleman
3. Eddie Collins
3. Phil Garner
4. Joe Gordon
6. Billy Martin

135. Who was the first player to homer in his first two World Series at-bats?

1. Bernie Carbo
2. Chuck Essegian
3. Andruw Jones
4. Benny Kauff
5. Gene Tenace

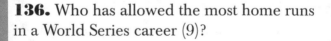

136. Who has allowed the most home runs in a World Series career (9)?

1. George Earnshaw
2. Catfish Hunter
3. Walter Johnson
4. Charlie Root
5. Red Ruffing
6. Rick Wise

137. Who holds the World Series record for consecutive errorless games at shortstop (21)?

1. Dave Bancroft
2. Johnny Logan
3. Roger Peckinpaugh
4. Pee Wee Reese
5. Phil Rizzuto
6. Ozzie Smith

138. Who is the most recent player to reach four career triples in World Series play?

1. George J. Burns
2. Tommy Davis
3. Lou Gehrig
4. Billy Johnson
5. Phil Rizzuto
6. George Rohe

139. Which pitcher holds the record for strikeouts in one World Series (35)?

1. Babe Adams
2. Whitey Ford
3. Bob Gibson
4. Jim Palmer
5. Tom Seaver
6. Todd Worrell

140. Who holds the record for most singles in one World Series (12)?

1. Lou Brock
2. Steve Garvey
3. Monte Irvin
4. Chief Meyers
5. Sam Rice
6. Jimmy Sebring

141. Who is the only outfielder to turn two double plays in one World Series game?

1. Ray Blades
2. Joe DiMaggio
3. Elston Howard
4. Willie McGee
5. Edd Roush

142. Which pitcher holds the World Series record for most strikeouts in relief in one game (11)?

1. Tex Carleton
2. Moe Drabowsky
3. Rollie Fingers
4. Dan Quisenberry
5. Vic Raschi
6. Todd Worrell

143. Who holds the World Series record for fewest putouts in a nine-inning game by a first baseman (1)?

1. Orlando Cepeda
2. Jiggs Donahue
3. Gil Hodges
4. Fred McGriff
5. Bill Skowron
6. Gene Tenace

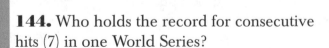

144. Who holds the record for consecutive hits (7) in one World Series?

1. Tommie Agee
2. Billy Hatcher
3. Gonzalo Marquez
4. Paul Molitor
5. Brooks Robinson
6. Frank Robinson

145. Who was the first American League batter to come to bat three times in one inning (1948)?

1. Ty Cobb
2. Joe DiMaggio
3. Moose Skowron
4. Ted Williams

146. Which catcher holds the record for most nine-inning no-hitters caught (4)?

1. Bob Boone
2. Roy Campanella
3. Del Crandall
4. Johnny Roseboro
5. Ray Schalk
6. Jeff Torborg

147. Who was the first major leaguer to be intentionally walked with the bases loaded?

1. Sam Crawford
2. Jimmie Foxx
3. Napoleon Lajoie
4. Babe Ruth

148. Which pitcher holds the NL and AL records for most games pitched in a season?

1. Sparky Lyle
2. Mike Marshall
3. Jesse Orosco
4. Bobby Thigpen
5. Hoyt Wilhelm
6. Mitch Williams

149. Who was the first bonus baby (young player given a large bonus to sign with his first major league team)?

1. Clint Hartung
2. Ralph Kiner
3. Pee Wee Reese
4. Dick Wakefield

★ ◆ ★ ◆ ★

150. Who wrote the poem "Casey at the Bat"?

1. Ring Lardner
2. Grantland Rice
3. Red Smith
4. Ernest Thayer
5. Earle Warren
6. Walt Whitman

151. Who is the only pitcher since the Cy Young Award was instituted in 1956 to have three 25-win seasons in which he was not the Cy Young winner?

1. Don Drysdale
2. Bob Gibson
3. Juan Marichal
4. Warren Spahn

152. What two players hold the major league record for most games played together for one team (2,015)?

1. Ernie Banks & Billy Williams
2. Mark Belanger & Brooks Robinson
3. Steve Garvey & Ron Cey
3. Ron Santo & Billy Williams
4. Lou Whitaker & Alan Trammell

153. Who are the only brothers to oppose each other as rookie starting pitchers in a game?

1. Bob & Ken Forsch
2. Greg & Mike Maddux
3. Pasqual & Melido Perez
4. Rick & Paul Reuschel

★ ◆ ★ ◆ ★

154. Who was the first player to win a Gold Glove in both the American and National Leagues?

1. Tommie Agee
2. Clete Boyer
3. Curt Flood
4. Graig Nettles
5. Bill Skowron
6. Devon White

155. Which pitcher hit the most batters with pitches in his career (206)?

1. Don Drysdale
2. Bob Gibson
3. Emerson Hawley
4. Walter Johnson
5. Sal Maglie
6. Warren Spahn

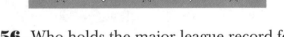

156. Who holds the major league record for saves by a rookie (36)?

1. Gregg Olson
2. Jeff Reardon
3. Lee Smith
4. Bobby Thigpen
5. Hoyt Wilhelm
6. Todd Worrell

157. Who holds the major league season record for times reaching base through catcher's interference (8)?

1. Dale Berra
2. Yogi Berra
3. Roberto Kelly
4. Pete Rose
5. Joe Sewell
6. Ted Williams

158. Who hit into the only triple play ever turned at Dodger Stadium?

1. Kurt Abbott
2. Billy Ashley
3. Sid Fernandez
4. Ken Landreaux
5. Greg Luzinski
6. Fernando Valenzuela

159. Who is the only player to get hits for two teams on the same day?

1. Delino DeShields
2. Forrest Jacobs
3. George Kell
4. Dale Long
5. Albie Pearson
6. Joel Youngblood

160. Who holds the major league record for most consecutive strikeouts in a game (10)?

1. Roger Clemens
2. Ron Davis
3. Joe Hoerner
4. Randy Myers
5. Nolan Ryan
6. Tom Seaver

161. Which team holds the major league record for most consecutive years without winning the league championship (52)?

1. Boston/Milwaukee Braves
2. Boston Red Sox
3. Chicago Cubs
4. Pittsburgh Pirates
5. St. Louis Browns/Baltimore Orioles
6. Washington Senators/Minnesota Twins

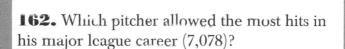

162. Which pitcher allowed the most hits in his major league career (7,078)?

1. Grover Alexander
2. Pud Galvin
3. Walter Johnson
4. Bobo Newsome
5. Jim Palmer
6. Cy Young

163. Who holds the Seattle Pilots' season and career record for home runs (25)?

1. Wayne Comer
2. Tommy Harper
3. Mike Hegan
4. Don Mincher

164. Which pitcher holds the Chicago Cubs' season record for strikeouts (274)?

1. Mordecai Brown
2. Ken Holtzman
3. Ferguson Jenkins
4. Greg Maddux
5. Rick Sutcliffe
6. Kerry Wood

165. Who holds the St. Louis Cardinals' career record for shutouts (56)?

1. Grover Cleveland Alexander
2. Dizzy Dean
3. Bob Gibson
4. Jack W. Taylor

166. Who holds the Philadelphia Phillies' season record for RBI (170)?

1. Dick Allen
2. Ed Delahanty
3. Del Ennis
4. Chuck Klein
5. Greg Luzinski
6. Mike Schmidt

167. Which batter holds the New York Giants' season record for bases on balls (144)?

1. Sid Gordon
2. George Kelly
3. Willie Mays
4. Eddie Stanky

168. John Olerud's .353 batting average in 1998 set a Mets record. Which Met had previously held the record with a .340 season?

1. Hubie Brooks
2. Buddy Harrelson
3. Keith Hernandez
4. Cleon Jones
5. Dave Magadan
6. Lee Mazzilli

169. Who holds the Houston Astros' season record for singles (160)?

1. Jose Cruz
2. Sonny Jackson
3. Joe Morgan
4. Doug Rader

170. Who holds the Los Angeles Dodgers' season record for starts by a pitcher (42)?

1. Al Downing
2. Don Drysdale
3. Sandy Koufax
4. Ramon Martinez
5. Andy Messersmith
6. Don Sutton

171. Who holds the major league career record for most times caught stealing?

1. Lou Brock
2. Brett Butler
3. Bert Campaneris
4. Ty Cobb
5. Rickey Henderson
6. Maury Wills

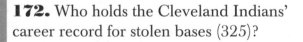

172. Who holds the Cleveland Indians' career record for stolen bases (325)?

1. Bobby Bonds
2. Lou Boudreau
3. Brett Butler
4. Shoeless Joe Jackson
5. Napoleon Lajoie
6. Kenny Lofton
7. Vic Wertz

173. Who holds the Colorado Rockies' season record for saves (25)?

1. Willie Blair
2. Greg Harris
3. Darren Holmes
4. Curt Leskanic
5. Steve Reed
6. Bruce Ruffin

174. Who holds the Chicago White Sox' career record for hits (2,749)?

1. Luis Aparicio
2. Luke Appling
3. Harold Baines
4. Eddie Collins
5. Nellie Fox
6. Joe Jackson

175. Who holds the Cincinnati Reds' season record for games pitched (90)?

1. Pedro Borbon
2. Rob Dibble
3. Wayne Granger
4. Randy Myers
5. Ted Power
6. Eppa Rixey

★ ◆ ★ ◆ ★

176. Who holds the Angels' career record for grand slams (7)?

1. Don Baylor
2. Brian Downing
3. Jim Fregosi
4. Johnny Ray
5. Joe Rudi
6. Leon Wagner

177. Who holds the Baltimore (AL franchise 1954–present) Orioles' season record for triples (12)?

1. Roberto Alomar
2. Brady Anderson
3. Luis Aparicio
4. Paul Blair
5. Rich Dauer
6. George Kell

★ ◆ ★ ◆ ★

178. Which batter holds the Seattle Mariners' season record for hit-by-pitch (17)?

1. Julio Cruz
2. Alvin Davis
3. Dan Meyer
4. Tom Paciorek
5. Jim Presley
6. Dave Valle

179. Who holds the Chicago Cubs' career record for doubles (530)?

1. Cap Anson
2. Ernie Banks
3. Frank Chance
4. Stan Hack
5. Ron Santo
6. Billy Williams

★ ◆ ★ ◆ ★

180. Which player holds the Dodgers' season record for games (165)?

1. Ron Cey
2. Tommie Davis
3. Steve Garvey
4. Gil Hodges
5. Bill Russell
6. Maury Wills

181. Who is the American League career saves leader (323)?

1. Dennis Eckersley
2. Rollie Fingers
3. Sparky Lyle
4. Dan Quisenberry

182. Who holds the major league season record (162 game season) for at-bats (705)?

1. Vince Coleman
2. Nomar Garciaparra
3. Rickey Henderson
4. Kirby Puckett
5. Juan Samuel
6. Willie Wilson

183. Which was the first team to have three players with 50 or more stolen bases in the same season?

1. Montreal Expos
2. Oakland A's
3. San Diego Padres
4. St. Louis Cardinals

★　◆　★　◆　★

184. Who holds the AL season record for runs (177)?

1. Rod Carew
2. Joe DiMaggio
3. Rickey Henderson
4. Babe Ruth
5. Willie Wilson
6. Ted Williams

185. Who holds the AL career record for the most pinch-hits (107)?

1. Gates Brown
2. Smokey Burgess
3. Luis Polonia
4. Elmer Valo

186. Who was the last Milwaukee Brewer to steal four bases in one game?

1. Jim Gantner
2. Marquis Grissom
3. Tommy Harper
4. John Jaha
5. Paul Molitor
6. Gary Sheffield

187. Who was the first switch-hitter with 100 hits from each side of the plate in one season?

1. Howard Johnson
2. Pete Rose
3. Garry Templeton
4. Willie Wilson

188. Who holds the National League record for home runs in his team's opening game of the season (3)?

1. Hank Aaron
2. Howard Johnson
3. Ralph Kiner
4. Karl Rhodes
5. Mike Schmidt
6. Hal Trosky

189. Who is the major league career leader in RBI (2,297)?

1. Hank Aaron
2. Lou Gehrig
3. Babe Ruth
4. Ted Williams

190. Who is the only American League player to ever have three hits in one inning?

1. Jerry Coleman
2. Johnny Hodapp
3. Sherm Lollar
4. Billy Martin
5. Russ Morman
6. Rusty Staub
7. Gene Stephens

191. Who is the major league career leader in losses by a pitcher (313)?

1. Pud Galvin
2. Walter Johnson
3. Jim Kaat
4. Bobo Newsom
5. Warren Spahn
6. Cy Young

192. Who is the NL career leader in triples (252)?

1. Max Carey
2. Stan Musial
3. Pete Rose
4. Honus Wagner
5. Maury Wills
6. Owen Wilson

193. Who holds the major league season record for most times hit by a pitch (50)?

1. Brady Anderson
2. Don Baylor
3. Rickey Henderson
4. Ron Hunt
5. Gene Larkin
6. Minnie Minoso

194. Who holds the American League career record for runs allowed (2,117)?

1. Walter Johnson
2. Jim Kaat
3. Red Ruffing
4. Ed Walsh
5. Wilbur Wood
6. Early Wynn

195. Who holds the National League season record for grounding into double plays (30)?

1. Hank Aaron
2. George Foster
3. Ken Hubbs
4. Ernie Lombardi
5. Willie Montanez
6. Dave Parker

196. Who was the first man to total three pinch-hit grand slams in his career?

1. Steve Braun
2. Gates Brown
3. Manny Mota
4. Ron Northey
5. Dusty Rhodes
6. Rusty Staub

197. Who is the National League career leader in bases on balls received (1,799)?

1. Hank Aaron
2. Barry Bonds
3. Gil Hodges
4. Joe Morgan
5. Mel Ott
6. Ed Stanky

198. Which pitcher holds the National League career record for strikeouts (4,000)?

1. Steve Carlton
2. Bob Gibson
3. Sandy Koufax
4. Nolan Ryan
5. Tom Seaver
6. Warren Spahn

199. Who holds the major league 162-game-season record for double plays by a third baseman (54)?

1. Wade Boggs
2. Clete Boyer
3. Graig Nettles
4. Brooks Robinson

★ ◆ ★ ◆ ★

200. Who holds the Mariners' rookie season record for home runs (27)?

1. Alvin Davis
2. Ken Griffey, Jr.
3. Dave Henderson
4. Edgar Martinez
5. Alex Rodriguez
6. Danny Tartabull

201. Who was the last player to have 7 hits in a 9-inning major league game?

1. Ty Cobb
2. Mickey Rivers
3. Aurelio Rodriguez
4. Rennie Stennett

202. Who was the last American League pitcher with five hits in a game?

1. Jim Lonborg
2. Dave McNally
3. Rick Rhoden
4. Red Ruffing
5. Babe Ruth
6. Mel Stottlemyre

203. Who holds the AL career record for total bases (5,862)?

1. Ty Cobb
2. Babe Ruth
3. Ted Williams
4. Carl Yastrzemski

204. Who holds the NL record for most consecutive games by a shortstop (584)?

1. Larry Bowa
2. Roy McMillan
3. Ozzie Smith
4. Arky Vaughan
5. Pee Wee Reese
6. Bobby Wine

205. Who is believed to be the career leader in the unofficial statistic of steals of home (50)?

1. Max Carey
2. Ty Cobb
3. Rickie Henderson
4. Jackie Robinson

★ ◆ ★ ◆ ★

206. Who was the first pitcher to appear in over a thousand games in a career of less than 20 seasons?

1. Dennis Eckersley
2. Rollie Fingers
3. Gene Garber
4. Mike Marshall
5. Lee Smith
6. Kent Tekulve

207. Who is the only AL player to hit for the cycle 3 times in his career?

1. Doc Cramer
2. Walt Dropo
3. Bob Meusel
4. Mickey Rivers

208. Who was the first 30-30 player (30 homers and 30 stolen bases in one season)?

1. Hank Aaron
2. Bobby Bonds
3. Tommy Harper
4. Mickey Mantle
5. Willie Mays
6. Joe Morgan
7. Kenny Williams

209. Who holds the major league first base record for most years leading his league in errors (7)?

1. Willie Aikens
2. Hal Chase
3. Dave Kingman
4. Dick Stuart

210. Who holds the major league record for consecutive stolen bases with no caught stealing (50)?

1. Vince Coleman
2. Rickey Henderson
3. Davey Lopes
4. Kevin McReynolds
5. Tim Raines
6. Willie Wilson

211. Who holds the major league record for most stolen bases in a season with no caught stealing (21)?

1. Vince Coleman
2. Rickey Henderson
3. Davey Lopes
4. Kevin McReynolds
5. Tim Raines
6. Willie Wilson

212. Who was the last batter to reach base on errors three times in one game?

1. Phil Bradley
2. Choo Choo Coleman
3. Rick Dempsey
4. Ray Durham
5. Steve Lyons
6. Mario Mendoza

213. Which batter holds the record for most consecutive times reaching base (16)?

1. Kiki Cuyler
2. Walt Dropo
3. Pedro Guerrero
4. Pinky Higgins
5. Davey Lopes
6. Ted Williams

214. Who holds the AL career record for most intentional bases on balls received (229)?

1. George Brett
2. Lou Gehrig
3. Reggie Jackson
4. Harmon Killebrew
5. Mickey Mantle
6. Eddie Murray
7. Ted Williams

215. Who holds the AL record for longest errorless game by a third baseman (25 innings)?

1. Bill Bradley
2. Dave Hansen
3. Jimmy Johnston
4. Vance Law
5. Don Money
6. Brooks Robinson

★ ◆ ★ ◆ ★

216. Who was the last major league pitcher with two complete-game victories in one day?

1. Grover Alexander
2. Herman Bell
3. Bill Doak
4. Dutch Levsen
5. Carl Mays
6. Joe McGinnity

217. Who pitched the first perfect game in American League history?

1. Jack Chesbro
2. Walter Johnson
3. Addie Joss
4. Cy Young

218. Which franchise holds the National League record for most last-place finishes (26)?

1. Brooklyn/Los Angeles Dodgers
2. Chicago Cubs
3. Cincinnati Reds
4. New York Mets
5. Philadelphia Phillies
6. Pittsburgh Pirates

219. Who holds the American League career record for putouts by an outfielder (6,794)?

1. Joe DiMaggio
2. Mickey Mantle
3. Tris Speaker
4. Carl Yastrzemski

220. Who holds the American League career record for errors by a first baseman (285)?

1. Bill Buckner
2. Norm Cash
3. Hal Chase
4. Boog Powell
5. Dick Stuart
6. Frank Thomas

221. Who holds the major league career for 1–0 games won by a pitcher (38)?

1. Whitey Ford
2. Walter Johnson
3. Sandy Koufax
4. Tom Seaver

222. Who holds the major league career for 1–0 games lost by a pitcher (26)?

1. Don Drysdale
2. Walter Johnson
3. Sandy Koufax
4. Jim Palmer
5. Nolan Ryan
6. Warren Spahn

223. Who holds the National League season record for slugging percentage by a switch-hitter (.621)?

1. Bobby Bonds
2. Ken Caminiti
3. Howard Johnson
4. Willie McGee

224. Who holds the National League career record for batting average (.359)?

1. Hugh Duffy
2. Rogers Hornsby
3. Wee Willie Keeler
4. Tony Gwynn
5. Stan Musial
6. Honus Wagner

225. Who played in the most seventh games of the World Series (8)?

1. Yogi Berra
2. Elston Howard
3. Mickey Mantle
4. Moose Skowron

226. Who holds the major league record for stolen bases in his rookie season (110)?

1. John Cangelosi
2. Vince Coleman
3. Rickey Henderson
4. Kenny Lofton
5. Davey Lopez
6. Harry Stovey
7. Maury Wills

227. Who holds the American League record for most years leading the league in caught stealing (6)?

1. Bobby Bonds
2. Brett Butler
3. Eddie Collins
4. Dom DiMaggio
5. Rickey Henderson
6. Minnie Minoso

★ ◆ ★ ◆ ★

228. Who was the first American Leaguer to hit a grand-slam home run?

1. Ty Cobb
2. Marty Kavanagh
3. Napoleon Lajoie
4. Herm McFarland
5. Ray Morehart
6. Kenny Williams

229. Who was the first major league player to hit a home run in a night game?

1. Lou Boudreau
2. Dolph Camilli
3. Babe Herman
4. Ducky Medwick
5. Johnny Mize
6. Johnny Pesky

230. Who was the first manager to be ejected from two games in one day by the umpires?

1. Charlie Comiskey
2. Connie Mack
3. John McGraw
4. Mel Ott
5. Paul Richards
6. Earl Weaver

231. Who holds the Milwaukee Brewers' career record for stolen bases (412)?

1. Rob Deer
2. Tommy Harper
3. Pat Listach
4. Paul Molitor
5. Don Money
6. Robin Yount

232. Off what pitcher did Roger Maris hit his 61st home run in 1961?

1. Jack Fisher
2. Paul Foytack
3. Eli Grba
4. Cal McLish
5. Billy Muffet
6. Tracy Stallard

233. Which pitcher holds the major league career record for grand slams allowed (10)?

1. Bert Blyleven
2. Roy Face
3. Bob Feller
4. Ned Garner
5. Jim Kaat
6. Nolan Ryan

234. Which pitcher is the active major league career leader in strikeouts?

1. Roger Clemens
2. Dennis Eckersley
3. Dwight Gooden
4. Orel Hershiser
5. Randy Johnson
6. Mark Langston

235. Who holds the National League record for most innings in a season without hitting a batter with a pitch (323)?

1. Steve Carlton
2. Sandy Koufax
3. Greg Maddux
4. Christy Mathewson

★　◆　★　◆　★

236. Who holds the National League career record for wild pitches (200)?

1. Rex Barney
2. Steve Carlton
3. Don Drysdale
4. Juan Marichal
5. Phil Niekro
6. Hoyt Wilhelm

237. Who was the first American League pitcher to strike out 4 batters in one inning?

1. Andy Hawkins
2. Walter Johnson
3. Guy Morton
4. Nolan Ryan

238. Who holds the American League career record for bases on balls allowed (1,775)?

1. Bert Blyleven
2. Walter Johnson
3. Jim Kaat
4. Red Ruffing
5. Nolan Ryan
6. Early Wynn

239. Who holds the major league season record for saves (57)?

1. Dennis Eckersley
2. Randy Myers
3. Lee Smith
4. Bobby Thigpen

240. Who holds the American League season record for wins by a pitcher (41)?

1. Jack Chesbro
2. Walter Johnson
3. Denny McLain
4. Eddie Plank
5. Cy Young
6. Rube Waddell

241. Who is the only pitcher to lead his league in winning percentage in five seasons?

1. Lefty Grove
2. Ron Guidry
3. Preacher Roe
4. Ed Ruelbach

242. Who is the relief pitcher who holds both the NL and AL season records for games pitched (106 and 89, respectively)?

1. Bill Campbell
2. Dennis Eckersley
3. Goose Gossage
4. Mike Marshall
5. Kent Tekulve
6. Hoyt Wilhelm

243. Walter Johnson set the major league record for games pitched with one team (802). Who is the only other pitcher to tie that mark?

1. Steve Carlton
2. Roy Face
3. Fernando Valenzuela
4. Cy Young

244. Who holds the American League rookie record for runs in a season (132)?

1. Joe DiMaggio
2. Nomar Garciaparra
3. Lou Gehrig
4. Rickey Henderson
5. Kenny Lofton
6. Ted Williams
7. Willie Wilson

245. Who was the first National Leaguer to hit 50 home runs in two seasons?

1. George Foster
2. Rogers Hornsby
3. Ralph Kiner
4. Willie Mays
5. Mel Ott
6. Mike Schmidt

246. Who was the first batter to hit 3 grand slams in one month?

1. Jimmie Foxx
2. Lou Gehrig
3. Tommy Henrich
4. Eddie Murray
5. Babe Ruth
6. Rudy York

247. Who holds the National League season record for total bases by a batter (450)?

1. Barry Bonds
2. Tommy Davis
3. Rogers Hornsby
4. Stan Musial
5. Willie Stargell
6. Larry Walker

248. Who was the first batter to have 6 RBI in an inning after the RBI became an official statistic in 1920?

1. Joe Astroth
2. Jim Ray Hart
3. Bob Johnson (Phi.)
4. Gil McDougald
5. Sam Mele
6. Boog Powell

249. Game-winning RBI was an official statistic from 1980 through 1988. Who holds the major league career record in this category (129)?

1. Jack Clark
2. Kirk Gibson
3. Keith Hernandez
4. Eddie Murray

250. Ted Williams set the American League season record for intentional walks (33) in 1957. Who is the only AL batter to tie this record?

1. Norm Cash
2. Al Kaline
3. Mickey Mantle
4. Roger Maris
5. John Olerud

251. Who holds the National League career record for strikeouts by a batter (1,936)?

1. Hank Aaron
2. Willie Mays
3. Wally Moon
4. Juan Samuel
5. Mike Schmidt
6. Willie Stargell

252. Who holds the major league record for most bases on balls received in a doubleheader (8)?

1. Max Bishop
2. Jack Clark
3. Clay Dalrymple
4. Johnny Mize
5. Mel Ott
6. Ted Williams

253. Who was the first player to have five hits in his major league debut?

1. Fred Clarke
2. Lou Gehrig
3. Joe Morgan
4. Cecil Travis

254. When Ted Williams missed winning the Triple Crown in 1949, when he led the AL in homers and RBI, who beat him out for the batting title by .00016 of a point?

1. Lou Boudreau
2. Bob Dillinger
3. Joe DiMaggio
4. George Kell
5. Johnny Pesky
6. Mickey Vernon

255. Who is the only National League manager to manage the same team four separate times?

1. Frank Chance
2. Danny Murtaugh
3. Bill Virdon
4. Leo Durocher

★ ◆ ★ ◆ ★

256. Who was the last catcher to win a major league batting average title?

1. Johnny Bench
2. Yogi Berra
3. Roy Campanella
4. Ernie Lombardi
5. Mike Piazza
6. Manny Sanguillen

257. Who was the last American League pitcher to steal home?

1. Harry Dorish
2. Red Faber
3. Dave McNally
4. Billy Pierce

258. Who was the first batter to homer in every major league park in use during his career?

1. Jimmie Foxx
2. Harry Heilmann
3. Napoleon Lajoie
4. Roger Maris
5. Frank Robinson
6. Babe Ruth

259. Who won the most Gold Gloves as a catcher (10)?

1. Johnny Bench
2. Bob Boone
3. Gary Carter
4. Jim Sundberg

260. Who was the first batter to lead the American League in home runs four years in a row?

1. Frank Baker
2. Ty Cobb
3. Harry Davis
4. Hank Greenberg
5. Babe Ruth
6. Ken Williams

261. Who was the first American League shortstop to hit .300 with 30 homers and 100 RBI in a season?

   1. Lou Boudreau
   2. Joe Cronin
   3. Cal Ripken
   4. Vern Stephens

262. Who is the youngest manager to start a season?

   1. Walter Alston
   2. Lou Boudreau
   3. Joe Cronin
   4. Bud Harrelson
   5. Tony LaRussa
   6. Roger Peckinpaugh
   7. Tom Sheehan

263. Mark McGwire's 162 walks in 1998 set an NL record. Who held the previous record with 151 free passes?

1. Hank Aaron
2. Barry Bonds
3. Bobby Bonds
4. Jack Clark
5. Pedro Guerrero

264. Which pitcher holds the National League career record for strikeouts by a righthander (3,272)?

1. Don Drysdale
2. Phil Niekro
3. Nolan Ryan
4. Tom Seaver
5. Don Sutton
6. Cy Young

265. Who was the first man to play for four American League teams in one season?

1. Pat Donahue
2. Frank Huelsman
3. Harry Lockhead
4. Bobo Newsome
5. Harry Simpson
6. Jim Whitney

266. Who was the first National Leaguer to strike out twice in one inning?

1. Hal Chase
2. Gil Hodges
3. Ernie Lombardi
4. Larry McLean
5. Pete Reiser
6. Edd Roush
7. Oscar Walker

267. Who holds the National League career record for games played at shortstop (2,511)?

1. Larry Bowa
2. Dick Groat
3. Rabbit Maranville
4. Roy McMillan
5. Pee Wee Reese
6. Ozzie Smith

268. Who holds the National League season record for total bases by a switch-hitter (369)?

1. Ken Caminiti
2. Rip Collins
3. Todd Hundley
4. Howard Johnson
5. Eddie Murray
6. Pete Rose
7. Reggie Smith

269. Who holds the major league career record for unassisted double plays by an outfielder (6)?

1. Paul Blair
2. Willie Mays
3. Tris Speaker
4. Mark Whiten
5. Dave Winfield

270. Who holds the American League record for consecutive scoreless innings by a pitcher $(55\frac{2}{3})$?

1. Dave Ferris
2. Lefty Grove
3. Joe Harris
4. Walter Johnson
5. Babe Ruth
6. Nolan Ryan

271. Who hit two home runs in a game the most times in a single season (11)?

1. Hank Greenberg
2. Mark McGwire
3. Babe Ruth
4. Sammy Sosa

272. Which batter had the most 200-hit seasons in the major leagues (10)?

1. Wade Boggs
2. Ty Cobb
3. Tony Gwynn
4. Rogers Hornsby
5. Pete Rose
6. George Sisler

273. Who spent the most years umpiring in the major leagues (37)?

1. Tommy Connolly
2. Don Denkinger
3. Doug Harvey
4. Bill Klem

274. Who was the first player in the American League to score 6 runs in a 9-inning game?

1. Ty Cobb
2. Sam Crawford
3. Napoleon Lajoie
4. Johnny Pesky
5. Sam Rice
6. Ted Williams

275. Who was the first player to hit 4 home runs in a game?

1. Lou Gehrig
2. George Hall
3. Bobby Lowe
4. Ned Williamson

276. Who holds the major league career record for double plays by a first baseman (2,044)?

1. Ferris Fain
2. Lou Gehrig
3. Charley Grimm
4. Keith Hernandez
5. Eddie Murray
6. Mickey Vernon

277. Who holds the American League career record for most times caught stealing in one inning (2)?

1. Don Baylor
2. Rickey Henderson
3. Pete Incaviglia
4. Gus Triandos

★ ◆ ★ ◆ ★

278. What batter holds the major league record for most seasons leading his league in bases on balls (11)?

1. Mickey Mantle
2. Babe Ruth
3. Mike Schmidt
4. Al Simmons
5. Ted Williams
6. Eddie Yost

279. What team holds the major league record for most consecutive home games lost in a season (20, in 1953)?

1. Chicago Cubs
2. Milwaukee Braves
3. Philadelphia Athletics
4. Philadelphia Phillies
5. St. Louis Browns
6. Washington Senators

280. Who was the last major leaguer to pitch an 18-inning shutout?

1. Carl Hubbell
2. Walter Johnson
3. Christy Mathewson
4. Joe McGinnity
5. Ed Summers
6. Monte Ward

281. Who holds the National League record for most home runs in a September (16)?

1. Bobby Bonds
2. Steve Garvey
3. Ralph Kiner
4. Willie Mays
5. Mike Schmidt
6. Willie Stargell

282. Who holds the major league career record for grand slams (23)?

1. Jimmie Foxx
2. Lou Gehrig
3. Jim Gentile
4. Willie McCovey
5. Eddie Murray
6. Babe Ruth
7. Ted Williams

283. Who holds the major league season record for balks (16)?

1. Steve Carlton
2. Rick Honeycutt
3. Tommy John
4. Vic Raschi
5. Dave Stewart
6. Gene Walter

284. Who was the last pitcher to shut out one club five times in the same season?

1. Steve Carlton
2. Bob Gibson
3. Larry Jaster
4. Sam McDowell
5. Tony Mullane
6. Jim Palmer

285. Which team holds the record for hitting the most home runs to start a game (3)?

1. Cubs
2. Dodgers
3. Giants
4. Mets
5. Padres
6. Yankees

286. Who holds the major league record for most teams managed (7)?

1. Frank Bancroft
2. Leo Durocher
3. Rogers Hornsby
4. Billy Martin
5. John McNamara
6. Dick Williams

287. Who holds the Los Angeles Dodgers' career hits record (2,091)?

1. Ron Cey
2. Willie Davis
3. Steve Garvey
4. Davey Lopes
5. Bill Russell
6. Maury Wills

288. Who is the major league career leader in runs scored (2,245)?

1. Hank Aaron
2. Ty Cobb
3. Rickey Henderson
4. Willie Mays
5. Pete Rose
6. Babe Ruth

289. Who holds the American League season record for hits by a switch-hitter (230)?

1. Mickey Mantle
2. Eddie Murray
3. George Sisler
4. Willie Wilson

290. Who holds the major league rookie season record for hits (223)?

1. Nomar Garciaparra
2. Tony Oliva
3. Jackie Robinson
4. Kevin Seitzer
5. Lloyd Waner
6. Ted Williams

291. Who holds the major league record for most years leading his league in being hit by pitches (10)?

1. Don Baylor
2. Ron Hunt
3. Jim Leyritz
4. Minnie Minoso

★ ◆ ★ ◆ ★

292. Who is the National League career leader in bases on balls allowed (1,717)?

1. Steve Carlton
2. Ferguson Jenkins
3. Amos Rusie
4. Nolan Ryan
5. Tom Seaver
6. Warren Spahn

293. Who holds the major league career record for most chances accepted by an outfielder (7,290)?

1. Richie Ashburn
2. Jose Cruz
3. Willie Mays
4. Tris Speaker

294. Who was the first National League first baseman to commit no errors in a season while playing at least 150 games (0)?

1. Sid Bream
2. Hal Chase
3. Steve Garvey
4. Keith Hernandez
5. Ted Kluszewski
6. Fred McGriff

295. Who holds the Los Angeles Dodgers' career record for grand slams (6)?

1. Kal Daniels
2. Steve Garvey
3. Mike Marshall
4. Mike Piazza

296. Who holds the Pittsburgh Pirates' career record for games played (2,528)?

1. Roberto Clemente
2. Ralph Kiner
3. Bill Mazeroski
4. Willie Stargell
5. Honus Wagner
6. Paul Waner

297. Who was the first major leaguer to receive two bases on balls in one inning?

1. Frankie Crosetti
2. Milt Galatzer
3. Otto Saltzgaver
4. George Selkirk
5. Eddie Stanky
6. Skeeter Webb

298. Which pitcher holds the New York Yankees' career record for losses (139)?

1. Jack Chesbro
2. Whitey Ford
3. Lefty Gomez
4. Red Ruffing
5. Bob Shawkey
6. Mel Stottlemyre, Sr.

299. Who holds the Chicago Cubs' career record for games played (2,528)?

1. Cap Anson
2. Ernie Banks
3. Frank Chance
4. Stan Hack
5. Ron Santo
6. Billy Williams

★ ◆ ★ ◆ ★

300. Who is the only National Leaguer to have grounded into four double plays in a nine inning game?

1. Rusty Kuntz
2. Greg Luzinski
3. Gary Roenicke
4. Garry Templeton
5. Joe Tinker
6. Joe Torre

301. Who holds the major league career record for years leading his league in stolen bases (12)?

1. Lou Brock
2. Max Carey
3. Ty Cobb
4. Eddie Collins
5. Rickey Henderson

302. Who holds the National League record for most times being hit by a pitch in a season (50)?

1. Cesar Cedeno
2. Andre Dawson
3. George Foster
4. Ron Hunt
5. Jeffrey Leonard
6. Rusty Staub

303. Who holds the American League season record for fewest times grounding into a double play in at least 150 games (0)?

1. Luis Aparicio
2. Al Bumbry
3. Al Kaline
4. Dick McAuliffe
5. Lonnie Smith
6. Kurt Stillwell

★　◆　★　◆　★

304. Who holds the San Francisco Giants' career record for games played (2,256)?

1. Bobby Bonds
2. Jack Clark
3. Jim Davenport
4. Juan Marichal
5. Willie Mays
6. Willie McCovey

305. Who holds the Cincinnati Reds' career record for grand slams (11)?

1. Johnny Bench
2. Eric Davis
3. George Foster
4. Ted Kluszewski
5. Joe Morgan
6. Tony Perez

306. Off which pitcher did Hank Aaron hit his 755th and last home run?

1. Dick Drago
2. Rich Gale
3. Ross Grimsley
4. Tom House
5. Jerry Reuss
6. Diego Segui

307. Who was the first Latin American to pitch a no-hitter in the major leagues?

1. Juan Guzman
2. Juan Marichal
3. Dennis Martinez
4. Camilo Pasqual

308. Who was the first major leaguer to hit for the cycle on Opening Day?

1. Hugh Duffy
2. Nap Lajoie
3. George Selkirk
4. Gee Walker
5. Maury Wills
6. Gene Woodling

309. Who is the only hitter ever to lead the National League in batting average while playing for an expansion team in its first season?

1. Richie Ashburn
2. Tommy Davis
3. Andres Galarraga
4. Tommy Harper

310. Who was the first player to win the MVP award while playing for the Houston Astros?

1. Jeff Bagwell
2. Jose Cruz
3. Joe Morgan
4. Mike Scott
5. Jimmy Wynn

311. In the first amateur draft in 1965, who was the first player selected?

1. Steve Garvey
2. Reggie Jackson
3. Rick Monday
4. Tom Seaver

312. When Nolan Ryan struck out his 383rd batter in 1973 to break Sandy Koufax's major league season mark, who was his victim?

1. Sal Bando
2. Rod Carew
3. Toby Harrah
4. Harmon Killebrew
5. Rich Reese
6. Cesar Tovar

313. Who holds the major league record for multiple-homer games (72)?

1. Hank Aaron
2. Jimmie Foxx
3. Willie Mays
4. Babe Ruth

314. When Casey Stengel managed the Yankees to the American League pennant in 1960, it was the tenth time he'd managed a team to the league championship; whose major league record did that tie?

1. Cap Anson
2. Miller Huggins
3. Connie Mack
4. John McGraw
5. Frank Seeley

315. Which team holds the major league record for consecutive games won in a season (26)?

1. Houston Astros
2. New York Giants
3. New York Yankees
4. Philadelphia Athletics
5. Oakland A's

316. Which Hall of Fame catcher holds the position record for most years leading his league in passed balls (9)?

1. Johnny Bench
2. Mickey Cochrane
3. Bill Dickey
4. Rick Ferrell
5. Ernie Lombardi
6. Ray Schalk

317. Which pitcher holds the National League career record for most shutouts by a lefthander (63)?

1. Steve Carlton
2. Carl Hubbell
3. Sandy Koufax
4. Eppa Rixey
5. Warren Spahn

318. Which pitcher holds the major league career record for most consecutive games lost to one club (13, amazingly, to the Cubs)?

1. John F. Coleman
2. Bob Forsch
3. Butch Metzger
4. Phil Nickro
5. Don Sutton
6. Eddie Yuhas

319. Who holds the National League record for most strikeouts by a batter in a double-header (7)?

1. Bobby Bonds
2. Rob Deer
3. Dave Kingman
4. Ron Swoboda
5. Mike Vail

320. Which pitcher holds the major league record for most starts in a season with no complete games (37)?

1. Stan Bahnsen
2. Steve Bedrosian
3. Tom Gordon
4. Kirk McCaskill
5. Kent Mercker
6. Rick Wise

321. Who was the first major leaguer to play 162 games in his rookie season?

1. Dick Allen
2. Ken Hubbs
3. Bobby Knoop
4. Jose Pagan
5. Pete Rose
6. Jake Wood

322. Which second baseman holds the major league record for most years leading his league in assists at that position (9)?

1. Eddie Collins
2. Nellie Fox
3. Frankie Frisch
4. Joe Gordon
5. Bill Mazeroski
6. Ryne Sandberg

323. Which pitcher holds the major league record for most home runs allowed in one game (7)?

1. Larry Benton
2. George Caster
3. George Cowley
4. Wayman Kerksieck
5. Joe Niekro
6. Charlie Sweeney

★ ◆ ★ ◆ ★

324. Who is the only manager to twice manage two different teams in the same year in the National League?

1. Ben Chapman
2. Leo Durocher
3. Rogers Hornsby
4. Ted Sullivan
5. Bill Virdon

325. Which team holds the American League season record for most consecutive games won with no tie games (19)?

1. Baltimore Orioles, 1983
2. New York Yankees, 1927
3. New York Yankees, 1947
4. Baltimore Orioles, 1969

326. Which team holds the major league season record for most double plays (217)?

1. Baltimore Orioles, 1997
2. Chicago Cubs, 1908
3. Chicago White Sox, 1959
4. Detroit Tigers, 1984
5. Philadelphia Athletics, 1949
6. St. Louis Cardinals, 1946

327. Who holds the major league season record for putouts by a catcher (1,135)?

1. Johnny Bench
2. Johnny Edwards
3. Bill Freehan
4. Ivan Rodriguez

328. Who holds the American League record for most singles in a rookie season (167)?

1. Wade Boggs
2. Ty Cobb
3. Harvey Kuenn
4. Don Mattingly
5. Al Simmons
6. Robin Yount

329. Which hurler holds the American League record for most runs allowed in his career?

1. Joe Niekro
2. Red Ruffing
3. Don Sutton
4. Wilbur Wood

330. Who was the first major leaguer to play all nine positions in one game?

1. Bert Campaneris
2. Bill Madlock
3. Sam Mertes
4. Jose Oquendo
5. Cesar Tovar
6. Maury Wills

331. Who holds the major league career record for sacrifice flies by a batter (123)?

1. Hank Aaron
2. Gil Hodges
3. Babe Ruth
4. Robin Yount

332. Which pitcher holds the American League season record for consecutive wins in relief (12)?

1. Luis Arroyo
2. Dennis Lamp
3. Sparky Lyle
4. Wilcy Moore
5. Dan Quisenberry
6. Arthur Rhodes

333. Who holds the National League career record for fielding percentage by a shortstop playing at least 1000 games (.980)?

1. Larry Bowa
2. Bud Harrelson
3. Rabbit Maranville
4. Ozzie Smith
5. Frank Tavares
6. Glenn Wright

334. Who holds the major league record for consecutive games lost by a pitcher (27)?

1. Terry Felton
2. Dave Morehead
3. Jack Nabors
4. Charlie Stecher
5. Don Sutton
6. Anthony Young

335. Who holds the major league career record for at-bats pitched (21,663)?

1. Steve Carlton
2. Walter Johnson
3. Robin Roberts
4. Nolan Ryan
5. Warren Spahn
6. Early Wynn

336. Which catcher holds the American League record for passed balls in a season (35)?

1. Marc Hill
2. Mickey Livingston
3. Geno Petralli
4. Wally Schang
5. Gus Triandos
6. Ivy Wingo

337. Who holds the major league record for chances accepted by a right fielder in a nine-inning game (12)?

1. Tony Armas
2. Lyman Bostock
3. Harry Schaefer
4. Casey Stengel
5. Dave Winfield

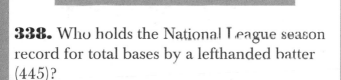

338. Who holds the National League season record for total bases by a lefthanded batter (445)?

1. Hank Aaron
2. Richie Allen
3. Rogers Hornsby
4. Chuck Klein
5. Mike Schmidt
6. Willie Stargell

339. Who was the first major league outfielder to play at least 150 games in a season and make no errors?

1. Brett Butler
2. Rocky Colavito
3. Brian Downing
4. Curt Flood
5. Danny Litwhiler
6. Terry Puhl

340. Who was the first major leaguer with three sacrifice flies in one game?

1. Sam Crawford
2. Napoleon Lajoie
3. Bob Meusel
4. Al Pilarcik
5. Harry Steinfeldt
6. Claudell Washington

341. Who holds the major league record for putouts by a shortstop in an extra-inning game (14)?

1. Luis Aparicio
2. Monte Cross
3. Bill Dahlen
4. Buck Herzog
5. Rabbit Maranville
6. Skeeter Webb

342. Who was the MVP of the 1983 World Series?

1. Mike Boddicker
2. Rick Dempsey
3. Scott McGregor
4. Eddie Murray
5. Cal Ripken, Jr.
6. Ken Singleton

343. Who holds the Minnesota Twins' career record for home runs by a lefthander (293)?

1. Rod Carew
2. Kent Hrbek
3. Harmon Killebrew
4. Tony Oliva

344. Who was the first batter to lead the National League in triples (14, 1876)?

1. Ross Barnes
2. Sam Crawford
3. Ed Delahanty
4. Wee Willie Keeler
5. Honus Wagner
6. Deacon White

345. Which pitcher holds the major league record for most consecutive wins by a rookie (17)?

1. Steve Avery
2. Pat Luby
3. Tom Seaver
4. George Wiltse

346. Who holds the National League season record for highest slugging percentage (.756)?

1. Hank Aaron
2. George Foster
3. Rogers Hornsby
4. Willie Mays
5. Stan Musial
6. Hack Wilson

347. Who holds the major league season record for games lost in relief (16)?

1. Ted Abernathy
2. Gene Garber
3. John Hiller
4. Mike Marshall

348. Who was the first batter to lead the American League in hits (1901)?

1. Ty Cobb
2. Patsy Dougherty
3. Charles Hickman
4. Napoleon Lajoie
5. Tris Speaker
6. George Stone

349. Who holds the major league career record for caught stealing (307)?

1. Lou Brock
2. Rickey Henderson
3. Miller Huggins
4. Maury Wills

350. Who holds the National League career record for most games pitched (1,050)?

1. Mike Marshall
2. Tug McGraw
3. Lee Smith
4. Bruce Sutter
5. Kent Tekulve
6. Hoyt Wilhelm

351. Who holds the American League first baseman's record for most innings played in one game (25)?

1. Lou Gehrig
2. George LaChance
3. Don Mattingly
4. Norm Sieburn
5. Ted Simmons
6. Mickey Vernon

★ ◆ ★ ◆ ★

352. Who holds the National League career record for games played at third base (2,212)?

1. Ron Cey
2. Stan Hack
3. Eddie Mathews
4. Ron Santo
5. Mike Schmidt
6. Pie Traynor

353. Who holds the major league record for most RBI in two consecutive games (15)?

1. Nate Colbert
2. Lou Gehrig
3. Tony Lazzeri
4. Stan Musial
5. Jim Tabor
6. Mark Whiten

354. Who is the Baltimore Orioles' career leader in stolen bases (252)?

1. Luis Aparicio
2. Al Bumbry
3. Don Buford
4. Bobby Grich
5. Brooks Robinson
6. Frank Robinson

355. Who was the first major league hitter with 8 at-bats in a nine-inning game?

1. Cap Anson
2. Ross Barnes
3. Joe Battin
4. Dave Force
5. Joe Quinn
6. Albert Spaulding

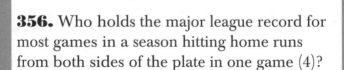

356. Who holds the major league record for most games in a season hitting home runs from both sides of the plate in one game (4)?

1. Roberto Alomar
2. Ken Caminiti
3. Howard Johnson
4. Mickey Mantle
5. Eddie Murray
6. Melvin Nieves

357. Which pitcher holds the Milwaukee Brewers' team record for consecutive games lost (10)?

1. Chris Bosio
2. Pete Broberg
3. Danny Darwin
4. Terry Felton
5. Moose Haas
6. Jim Slaton

358. Which was the last major league team to lose a game by forfeit (1979)?

1. Chicago Cubs
2. Chicago White Sox
4. Los Angeles Dodgers
5. Montreal Expos
7. Texas Rangers
8. Toronto Blue Jays

359. Who pitched the first no-hitter in major league history?

1. Jack Chesbro
2. Candy Cummings
3. Guy Hecker
4. Tony Mullane
5. Lee Richmond
6. Cy Young

360. Who was the first batter to have 12 consecutive hits with no walks included in the streak?

1. Don Baylor
2. Sam Crawford
3. Joe DiMaggio
4. Walt Dropo
5. Pinky Higgins
6. John Olerud

361. Who is the only player in National League history to hit for the cycle three times in his career?

1. Lou Brock
2. Babe Herman
3. Chuck Klein
4. Honus Wagner

362. Who was the last player to have two hits in an inning in his major league debut?

1. Roberto Alomar
2. Bret Boone
3. Chad Kreuter
4. Russ Mormon
5. Alex Ochoa
6. Ted Williams

363. Which pitcher holds the American League career record for most consecutive starting assignments (515)?

1. Roger Clemens
2. Jack Morris
3. Nolan Ryan
4. Dave Stewart

364. Which pitcher holds the American League career record for most shutouts won or tied by a lefthander (64)?

1. Steve Carlton
2. Walter Johnson
3. Lefty Grove
4. Eddie Plank
5. Babe Ruth
6. Warren Spahn

365. Who holds the major league record for most times caught stealing in his rookie season (25)?

1. Vince Coleman
2. Rickey Henderson
3. Goldie Rapp
4. Maury Wills

366. Which team was the last in the majors to win a game by overcoming a 12-run deficit?

1. Athletics
2. Cardinals
3. Cubs
4. Giants
5. Mariners
6. Rockies

367. Who holds the major league career record for putouts by an outfielder (7,095)?

1. Richie Ashburn
2. Willie Mays
3. Vada Pinson
4. Tris Speaker
5. Zack Wheat
6. Carl Yastrzemski

368. Which of these National Leaguers *didn't* catch three no-hitters?

1. Roy Campanella
2. Del Crandall
3. John Roseboro
4. Alan Ashby

369. Who holds the Twins' career record for runs (1,071)?

1. Rod Carew
2. Gary Gaetti
3. Kent Hrbek
4. Harmon Killebrew
5. Kirby Puckett
6. Cesar Tovar

370. Who holds the American League pitchers' record for most times leading the league in assists (6)?

1. Walter Johnson
2. Jim Kaat
3. Bob Lemon
4. Jim Perry
5. Ed Walsh
6. Early Wynn

371. Who was the last National Leaguer to lead the league in RBI three years in a row?

1. Hank Aaron
2. George Foster
3. Joe Medwick
4. Stan Musial
5. Mike Schmidt
6. Hack Wilson

372. Among pitchers with at least 200 career decision, who has the highest winning percentage (.690)?

1. Whitey Ford
2. Lefty Grove
3. Ron Guidry
4. Christy Mathewson
5. Dazzy Vance
6. Cy Young

373. Who holds the American League career record for assists by a shortstop (8,016)?

1. Luis Aparicio
2. Luke Appling
3. Bucky Dent
4. Cal Ripken Jr.
5. Phil Rizzuto
6. Joe Sewell

374. Who holds the American League record for most runs scored in a doubleheader (9)?

1. Mel Almeda
2. Joe DiMaggio
3. George Gore
4. Mickey Mantle
5. Rick Monday
6. Red Rolfe

375. Who was the last pitcher to pitch for four major league clubs in one season?

1. Willie Banks
2. Ted Gray
3. Willis Hudlin
4. Mike Kilkenny
5. Bob L. Miller
6. Elias Sosa

376. Which team holds the major league record for hits in a season (1,783)?

1. Athletics
2. Cubs
3. Mets
4. Pirates
5. Red Sox
6. Rockies

377. Who holds the major league season record for runs scored by a switch-hitter (140)?

1. Max Carey
2. Vince Coleman
3. Rickie Henderson
4. Howard Johnson
5. Pete Rose
6. George Sisler

378. Which team has won the most League Championship Series games (23)?

1. Baltimore Orioles
2. Cincinnati Reds
3. Los Angeles Dodgers
4. New York Yankees
5. Oakland A's
6. Pittsburgh Pirates

379. Who holds the Chicago White Sox career record for complete games (356)?

1. Red Faber
2. Ted Lyons
3. Ed Walsh
4. Wilbur Wood

380. Who holds the major league record for most consecutive home runs allowed in an inning (4)?

1. Dave Dravecky
2. Kevin Foster
3. Paul Foytack
4. Catfish Hunter
5. Mike Morgan
6. Mike Moore

381. Who are the only brothers to face each other in their rookie seasons?

1. Paul and Jay Dean
2. Bob and Ken Forsch
3. Greg and Mike Maddux
4. Joe and Phil Niekro

382. Who holds the Kansas City Royals' career record for most grand slams (6)?

1. Steve Balboni
2. George Brett
3. John Mayberry
4. Hal McRae
5. Amos Otis
6. Frank White

383. Who pitched the first no-hitter in National League history (1876)?

1. George Bradley
2. Larry Corcoran
3. Pud Galvin
4. Hoss Radbourn

384. Who was the only hitter from 1907 through 1919 to win an American League batting title besides Ty Cobb?

1. Harry Heilmann
2. Joe Jackson
3. Sam Rice
4. George Sisler
5. Tris Speaker
6. George Stone

385. Who holds the major league record for most consecutive games played at second base (798)?

1. Dave Cash
2. Nellie Fox
3. Jim Gantner
4. Ryne Sandberg

386. Who holds the Milwaukee Brewers' season record for home runs (45)?

1. Hank Aaron
2. Cecil Cooper
3. Ben Oglivie
4. Gorman Thomas
5. Greg Vaughn
6. Robin Yount

387. When is the earliest date the American League pennant has ever been clinched (NY Yankees, 1941)?

1. August 30
2. September 2
3. September 3
4. September 4
5. September 7
6. September 8

★ ◆ ★ ◆ ★

388. Who is the only American Leaguer to win 10 Gold Gloves as an outfielder?

1. Paul Blair
2. Dom DiMaggio
3. Dwight Evans
4. Al Kaline
5. Fred Lynn
6. Carl Yastrzemski

389. Who holds the major league rookie record for highest slugging average in a minimum of 100 games (.621)?

1. George Brett
2. Joe Charboneau
3. Elmer Flick
4. Mark McGwire
5. Juan Samuel
6. George Watkins

★　◆　★　◆　★

390. Who holds the New York Mets season record for total bases (327)?

1. Tommie Agee
2. Bernard Gilkey
3. Todd Hundley
4. Lance Johnson
5. Cleon Jones
6. Darryl Strawberry

391. Who holds the Detroit Tigers career record for strikeouts by a pitcher (2,679)?

1. Joe Coleman, Jr.
2. Bill Donovan
3. Mickey Lolich
4. Denny McLain
5. Jack Morris
6. Hal Newhouser

392. Who holds the National League rookie season record for bases on balls received (100)?

1. Fred Clarke
2. Jake Daubert
3. Jim Gilliam
4. Mike Schmidt
5. Bill Terry
6. Jim Wynn

393. Who holds the major league season record for pinch-hits (28)?

1. Gates Brown
2. Ed Coleman
3. Manny Mota
4. Jimmy Ryan
5. Rusty Staub
6. John Vander Wal

394. Who holds the major league record for most seasons leading his league in games pitched (7)?

1. Bill Campbell
2. Roy Face
3. Fred Marberry
4. Mike Marshall
5. Joe McGinnity
6. Hoyt Wilhelm

395. Who holds the Atlanta Braves career record for triples (40)?

1. Hank Aaron
2. Rico Carty
3. Ralph Garr
4. Eddie Mathews
5. Dale Murphy
6. Otis Nixon

★ ◆ ★ ◆ ★

396. Which company manufactured the Bill Doak model baseball glove, the first to have a natural pocket whose size could be adjusted by leather laces?

1. Nike
2. Rawlings
3. Spalding
4. Wilson

397. Who is the only pitcher to strike out 300 batters in a season after the age of 40?

1. Steve Carlton
2. Dennis Martinez
3. Nolan Ryan
4. Tom Seaver

398. Which manager holds the major league record for most consecutive years managed without winning a championship (23)?

1. Bobby Cox
2. Leo Durocher
3. Connie Mack
4. Gene Mauch
5. John McGraw
6. Chuck Tanner

399. Who holds the major league career record for putouts by a shortstop (5,133)?

1. Luis Aparicio
2. Rabbit Maranville
3. Phil Rizzuto
4. Ozzie Smith

400. Who was the first black pitcher in the major leagues after Jackie Robinson broke the color line in 1947?

1. Dan Bankhead
2. Vida Blue
3. Bob Gibson
4. Don Newcombe
5. Satchel Paige
6. Ted "Double Duty" Radcliffe

401. Who was the first minor leaguer purchased by a major league team for $100,000?

1. Jake Bentley
2. Lefty Grove
3. Willie Kamm
4. Babe Ruth

402. Who holds the American League season record for most earned runs allowed (186)?

1. Don Larsen
2. Bobo Newsom
3. Red Ruffing
4. Mike Torrez
5. Steve Trout
6. Wilbut Wood

403. Who was the last major leaguer to homer in four consecutive at-bats in one game?

1. Rocky Colavito
2. Lou Gehrig
3. Don Mattingly
4. Mike Schmidt

★ ◆ ★ ◆ ★

404. Who holds the major league season record for most at-bats without a home run (672)?

1. Mark Belanger
2. Doc Cramer
3. Duane Kuiper
4. Rabbit Maranville
5. Joe Sewell
6. Ozzie Smith

405. Which major league franchise has won the most games in history?

1. Braves
2. Cardinals
3. Cubs
4. Giants
5. Pirates
6. Yankees

406. Who holds the major league career record for putouts by a catcher (11,785)?

1. Johnny Bench
2. Yogi Berra
3. Bob Boone
4. Gary Carter
5. Bill Dickey
6. Carlton Fisk

407. Who holds the major league record for most years played by a non-pitcher (26)?

1. Ty Cobb
2. Eddie Collins
3. Rabbit Maranville
4. Deacon McGuire
5. Bobby Wallace
6. Carl Yastrzemski

408. Who was the first major leaguer to hit three home runs in a nine-inning game?

1. Ross Barnes
2. Irv Beck
3. Buck Freeman
4. George Hall
5. Bobby Lowe
6. Ned Williamson

409. Who holds the major league career record for most grand slams allowed (10)?

1. Bert Blyleven
2. Jerry Reuss
3. Robin Roberts
4. Nolan Ryan
5. Warren Spahn
6. Frank Tanana

410. Which team holds the major league season record for wins (116)?

1. Atlanta Braves
2. Boston Red Sox
3. Chicago Cubs
4. Cleveland Indians
5. New York Yankees
6. Philadelphia Athletics

411. Who holds the National League season record for most times reaching base on catcher's interference (7)?

1. Jay Bell
2. Dale Berra
3. Pat Corrales
4. Jerry Grote
5. Bill McKechnie
6. Andy Pafko

★　◆　★　◆　★

412. Who was the first player to lead the American League in triples (1901)?

1. Sam Crawford
2. Elmer Flick
3. Fielder Jones
4. Socks Seybold
5. Chick Stahl
6. Jimmy Williams

413. Who holds the major league season record for most home runs hit at home against one club (10)?

1. Joe Adcock
2. Rip Collins
3. Harry Heilmann
4. Ted Kluszewski
5. Willie Mays
6. Gus Zernial

★ ◆ ★ ◆ ★

414. Who holds the National League record for consecutive games played (1,207)?

1. Ernie Banks
2. Steve Garvey
3. Willie McCovey
4. Dale Murphy
5. Stan Musial
6. Billy Williams

415. Who was the last player to lead his league in at-bats three consecutive years?

1. Dave Cash
2. Doc Cramer
3. Rickey Henderson
4. Bobby Richardson

416. Who is the only player to twice lead his league in at-bats three consecutive years?

1. Lou Brock
2. Dave Cash
3. Doc Cramer
4. Sam Crawford
5. Rickey Henderson
6. Bobby Richardson

417. Who is the only batter to score 150 or more runs in a season six times?

1. Ty Cobb
2. Billy Hamilton
3. Stan Musial
4. Babe Ruth

418. Who holds the Yankees team record for most strikeouts in a season by a batter (156)?

1. Reggie Jackson
2. Tony Lazzeri
3. Mickey Mantle
4. Babe Ruth
5. Danny Tartabull
6. Dave Winfield

419. How many times have the Mets won 100 games or more in a season?

1. 1
2. 2
3. 3
4. 4

420. Which pitcher holds the second Washington Senators (1961–1971) career records for wins (49)?

1. Dick Bosman
2. Bennie Daniels
3. Darold Knowles
4. Denny McLain
5. Phil Ortega
6. Camilio Pascual

421. Who holds the Oakland A's career record for doubles?

1. Sal Bando
2. Rickey Henderson
3. Mark McGwire
4. Joe Rudi

422. Who holds the New York Giants career record for total bases (5,041)?

1. George Davis
2. Willie Mays
3. Irish Meusel
4. Mel Ott
5. Bill Terry
6. Bobby Thomson

423. Who holds the major league record for most hits in his rookie season (223)?

1. Dale Alexander
2. Wade Boggs
3. Lefty O'Doul
4. Tony Oliva
5. Lloyd Waner
6. Paul Waner

424. Which pitcher holds the major league record for most season openers won (9)?

1. Grover Alexander
2. Bob Gibson
3. Lefty Grove
4. Walter Johnson
5. Tom Seaver
6. Warren Spahn

425. Who holds the major league record for fewest errors in a season (150 or more games played) by a shortstop (3)?

1. Luis Aparicio
2. Larry Bowa
3. Ozzie Guillen
4. Don Kessinger
5. Cal Ripken, Jr.
6. Ozzie Smith

426. Who is the only batter with 10 seasons of 200 or more hits?

1. Wade Boggs
2. George Brett
3. Ty Cobb
4. Tony Gwynn
5. Willie Keeler
6. Pete Rose

427. Who holds the major league career record (since 1900) for putouts by a pitcher (387)?

1. Bert Blyleven
2. Walter Johnson
3. Christy Mathewson
4. Jack Morris
5. Phil Niekro
6. Vic Willis

428. Who holds the major league record for most consecutive pinch-hits (9)?

1. Smokey Burgess
2. Randy Bush
3. Dave Hansen
4. Manny Mota
5. Albie Pearson
6. Dave Philley

429. Who holds the Phillies season record for most grand slams hit (4)?

1. Richie Allen
2. Vince DiMaggio
3. Dave Hollins
4. Chuck Klein
5. Willie Montanez
6. Mike Schmidt

430. Who holds the National League season record (since 1900) for most wins by a pitcher (37)?

1. Grover Alexander
2. Dizzy Dean
3. Juan Marichal
4. Christy Mathewson
5. Ed Ruelbach
6. Warren Spahn

431. Who holds the major league career record for doubles (793)?

1. Hank Aaron
2. George Brett
3. Willie Mays
4. Stan Musial
5. Pete Rose
6. Tris Speaker

432. Who holds the major league season record for singles by a switch-hitter (184)?

1. Ken Caminiti
2. Chili Davis
3. Pete Rose
4. Wally Schang
5. Reggie Smith
6. Willie Wilson

433. Who holds the major league career record for most home runs hit as a third baseman (509)?

1. Home Run Baker
2. Eddie Mathews
3. Al Rosen
4. Mike Schmidt

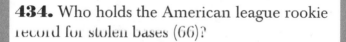

434. Who holds the American league rookie record for stolen bases (66)?

1. Rickey Henderson
2. Chuck Knoblauch
3. Pat Listach
4. Kenny Lofton
5. Harold Reynolds
6. Herb Washington

435. What is the only major league team to finish last in its league seven consecutive years?

1. Philadelphia Athletics
2. Philadelphia Phillies
3. Washington Senators
4. Seattle Mariners

436. Who holds the American League record for consecutive scoreless innings pitched by a lefthander (45)?

1. Mike Cuellar
2. Dave Ferriss
3. Ron Guidry
4. Joe Harris
5. Walter Johnson
6. Doc White

437. Who holds the major league career record for most home runs hit as a pitcher (37)?

1. Don Drysdale
2. Wes Ferrell
3. Babe Ruth
4. Warren Spahn

438. Who is the only batter with five major league seasons of 400 or more total bases?

1. Lou Gehrig
2. Jimmie Foxx
3. Rogers Hornsby
4. Stan Musial
5. Babe Ruth
6. Ted Williams

439. Who is the only pitcher to lead his league in earned run average five years in a row?

1. Grover Alexander
2. Lefty Grove
3. Sandy Koufax
4. Greg Maddux

440. Who is the only batter to lead his league seven consecutive years in hit-by-pitch?

1. Dusty Baker
2. Don Baylor
3. Ron Hunt
4. Minnie Minoso
5. Dave Parker
6. Pete Rose

441. Which pitcher holds the major league season record for highest winning percentage by a 20-game winner (.893)?

1. Jack Chesbro
2. Dwight Gooden
3. Lefty Grove
4. Ron Guidry
5. Christy Mathewson

442. Who holds the major league record for lowest stolen base total by the league leader (15)?

1. Luis Aparicio
2. Dom DiMaggio
3. Stan Hack
4. Mickey Mantle
5. Willie Mays
6. Jack Pitler

443. Who holds the American League career record for starts by a pitcher (666)?

1. Jack Chesbro
2. Lefty Grove
3. Walter Johnson
4. Jack Morris
5. Luis Tiant
6. Cy Young

444. Who holds the major league record for most bases on balls received in a rookie season (107)?

1. Barry Bonds
2. Mel Ott
3. Eddie Stanky
4. Frank Thomas
5. Ted Williams
6. Eddie Yost

445. Who holds the major league record for most total bases in a game (18)?

1. Joe Adcock
2. Ty Cobb
3. Lou Gehrig
4. Mark McGwire
5. Jim Seerey
6. Ted Williams

446. Who was the first batter to hit three triples in a nine-inning American League game?

1. Ty Cobb
2. Frank Dillon
3. Elmer Flick
4. Buck Freeman
5. Herm McFarland
6. Sammy Strang

447. Among active major leaguers, who has hit .300 in the most seasons (16)?

1. Wade Boggs
2. Tony Gwynn
3. Wally Joyner
4. Barry Larkin
5. Edgar Martinez
6. Cal Ripken

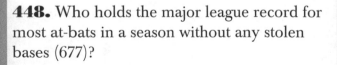

448. Who holds the major league record for most at-bats in a season without any stolen bases (677)?

1. Smokey Burgess
2. Brian Downing
3. Deron Johnson
4. Ernie Lombardi
5. Don Mattingly
6. Ken Singleton

449. Who holds the major league season record for most innings pitched in relief (208)?

1. Jack Aker
2. Bill Campbell
3. Sparky Lyle
4. Mike Marshall
5. Kent Tekulve
6. Hoyt Wilhelm

450. Who holds the major league record for most consecutive games played by a third baseman (576)?

1. Harlond Clift
2. George Kell
3. Eddie Mathews
4. Brooks Robinson
5. Mike Schmidt
6. Eddie Yost

451. After the RBI became an official statistic in 1920, who was the first Triple Crown winner?

1. Jimmie Foxx
2. Rogers Hornsby
3. Chuck Klein
4. Joe Medwick

★ ◆ ★ ◆ ★

452. Who holds the major league record for longest batting streak from the start of a season (44 games)?

1. George Brett
2. Bill Dahlen
3. Joe DiMaggio
4. Willie Keeler
5. Pete Rose
6. Carl Yazstrzemski

453. Which pitcher holds the Toronto Blue Jays season record for strikeouts (292)?

1. Roger Clemens
2. Juan Guzman
3. Jack Morris
4. Dave Stieb

454. Entering the 1998 season, which hitter held the Texas Rangers' career record for most strikeouts (788)?

1. Jeff Burroughs
2. Juan Gonzalez
3. Pete Incaviglia
4. Mickey Rivers
5. Ivan Rodriguez
6. Ruben Sierra

455. Who has the longest hitting streak in Seattle Mariners history (24 games)?

1. Joey Cora
2. Ken Griffey, Jr.
3. Edgar Martinez
4. Harold Reynolds
5. Alex Rodriguez
6. Paul Sorrento

★　◆　★　◆　★

456. Which pitcher is the Angels' career leader in wins (153)?

1. Bert Blyleven
2. Chuck Finley
3. Kirk McCaskill
4. Nolan Ryan
5. Frank Tanana
6. Mike Witt

457. Which pitcher holds the Atlanta Braves season record for wins (24)?

1. Steve Avery
2. Tony Cloninger
3. Tom Glavine
4. Greg Maddux
5. Phil Niekro
6. John Smoltz

458. Who is the Colorado Rockies career leader in runs scored (561)?

1. Dante Bichette
2. Ellis Burks
3. Vinny Castilla
4. Andres Galarraga
5. Larry Walker
6. Eric Young

459. Which pitcher holds the Florida Marlins career record for games won (33)?

1. Jack Armstrong
2. Kevin Brown
3. Charlie Hough
4. Al Leiter
5. Pat Rapp

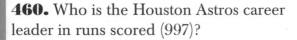

460. Who is the Houston Astros career leader in runs scored (997)?

1. Jeff Bagwell
2. Craig Biggio
3. Cesar Cedeno
4. Jose Cruz
5. Glenn Davis
6. Lee May
7. Doug Rader
8. Jimmy Wynn

461. Which pitcher holds the Los Angeles Dodgers career record for strikeouts (2,696)?

1. Tom Candiotti
2. Don Drysdale
3. Orel Hershiser
4. Sandy Koufax
5. Ramon Martinez
6. Don Sutton

162. Which pitcher holds the Montreal Expos record for most strikeouts in a game (18)?

1. Ross Grimsley
2. Bill Gullickson
3. Pedro Martinez
4. Carlos Perez
5. Steve Rogers
6. Bill Stoneman

463. Which pitcher holds the San Diego Padres career record for strikeouts (1,036)?

1. Andy Benes
2. Mark Davis
3. Randy Jones
4. Joe Niekro
5. Gaylord Perry
6. Eric Show

464. What is the major league record for most pitchers used by one team in a nine-inning game?

1. 6
2. 7
3. 8
4. 9
5. 11

465. Which major league team has spent the most years in the same city (123)?

1. Chicago Cubs
2. Cincinnati Reds
3. Philadelphia Phillies
4. Pittsburgh Pirates

466. Who was the first National Leaguer to play 162 games in his rookie season?

1. Richie Allen
2. Keith Hernandez
3. Ken Hubbs
4. Frank Robinson
5. Pete Rose
6. Joe Torre

467. Who holds the National League season record for at-bats (701)?

1. Lou Brock
2. Willie McGee
3. Juan Samuel
4. Mookie Wilson

468. Who is the only National Leaguer to score 150 or more runs in a season twice in the 20th century?

1. Willie Davis
2. Rogers Hornsby
3. Chuck Klein
4. Mel Ott
5. Tim Raines
6. Hack Wilson

469. Who is the only major leaguer to lead his league in hits eight times?

1. Ty Cobb
2. Hugh Duffy
3. Rogers Hornsby
4. Pete Rose

470. Who is the only player in American League history with five hits in his first career game?

1. Nellie Fox
2. Billy Herman
3. Fred Lynn
4. Kirby Puckett
5. Gene Tenace
6. Cecil Travis

471. Which team holds the major league record for most runners left on base in a season (1,334 in 1941)?

1. Chicago Cubs
2. New York Yankees
3. St. Louis Browns
4. Washington Senators

★　◆　★　◆　★

472. Which team holds the major league record for most home runs hit in a season (264 in 1997)?

1. Colorado Rockies
2. Baltimore Orioles
3. Los Angeles Dodgers
4. New York Yankees
5. Seattle Mariners
6. Texas Rangers

473. Who holds the major league record for most RBI by a rookie (145)?

1. Wally Berger
2. Tommy Davis
3. Joe DiMaggio
4. Willie McCovey
5. Frank Thomas
6. Ted Williams

474. Which pitcher holds the major league record for consecutive strikeouts in a game (10)?

1. Roger Clemens
2. Clay Kirby
3. Bob Gibson
4. Pedro Martinez
5. Nolan Ryan
6. Tom Seaver

475. Who holds the major league record for most games played at first base (2,413)?

1. Jake Beckley
2. Steve Garvey
3. Charlie Grimm
4. Eddie Murray
5. Vic Power
6. Mickey Vernon

476. Which pitcher is the active leader in ERA among pitchers with 3,000-plus innings (2.95)?

1. Roger Clemens
2. Dennis Eckersley
3. Dwight Gooden
4. Randy Johnson
5. Mark Langston
6. Dennis Martinez

477. Albert Belle set a White Sox record with 48 doubles in 1998. Whose record did he break?

1. Luis Aparicio
2. Luke Appling
3. Harold Baines
4. Nellie Fox
5. Shoeless Joe Jackson
6. Frank Thomas

478. Who holds the Oakland A's season record for total bases (347)?

1. Tony Armas
2. Jose Canseco
3. Reggie Jackson
4. Dave Kingman
5. Mark McGwire
6. Gene Tenace

479. Who holds the Atlanta Braves season record for batting average (.366)?

1. Felipe Alou
2. Hank Aaron
3. Rico Carty
4. Ralph Garr
5. Dale Murphy
6. Otis Nixon

480. Who has the longest batting streak in Florida Marlins history (22 games)?

1. Alex Aria
2. Chuck Carr
3. Greg Colbrunn
4. Jeff Conine
5. Tommy Gregg
6. Edgar Renteria

481. Who holds the Atlanta Braves career record for runs batted in (1,143)?

1. Hank Aaron
2. Bob Horner
3. Chipper Jones
4. Dale Murphy

482. Who holds the New York Yankees career record for stolen bases (326)?

1. Ben Chapman
2. Earle Combs
3. Rickey Henderson
4. Mickey Mantle
5. Mickey Rivers
6. Bernie Williams

483. Who holds the Florida Marlins career record for runs scored (344)?

1. Chuck Carr
2. Jeff Conine
3. Edgar Renteria
4. Gary Sheffield

484. Which pitcher holds the New York Mets' season record for strikeouts (289)?

1. Dave Cone
2. Ron Darling
3. Sid Fernandez
4. Dwight Gooden
5. Nolan Ryan
6. Tom Seaver

485. Which pitcher holds the Chicago White Sox career record for victories (260)?

1. Red Faber
2. Ted Lyons
3. Ed Walsh
4. Wilbur Wood

486. When was the last time the Chicago Cubs played in the World Series?

1. 1908
2. 1932
3. 1934
4. 1945
5. 1984
6. 1989

487. Who holds the Seattle Mariners career record for doubles (237)?

1. Alvin Davis
2. Ken Griffey, Jr.
3. Edgar Martinez
4. Harold Reynolds

488. Who holds the Cincinnati Reds career record for games pitched (531)?

1. Pedro Borbon
2. Tom Browning
3. Wayne Granger
4. Sparky Lyle
5. Eppa Rixey
6. Bucky Walters

489. Which pitcher holds the Colorado Rockies career record for victories (39)?

1. Roger Bailey
2. Armando Reynoso
3. Kevin Ritz
4. Bruce Ruffin

490. Who holds the Oakland A's season record for runs scored (123)?

1. Bert Campaneris
2. Jose Canseco
3. Dave Henderson
4. Rickey Henderson
5. Reggie Jackson
6. Carney Lansford
7. Joe Rudi

491. What year did the Houston Astros first have a winning record?

1. 1968
2. 1969
3. 1972
4. 1973
5. 1979
6. 1980

492. Who holds the Minnesota Twins career record for most seasons played (15)?

1. Rod Carew
2. Gary Gaetti
3. Kent Hrbek
4. Harmon Killebrew
5. Tony Oliva
6. Kirby Puckett

493. Who holds the Los Angeles Dodgers career record for home runs (228)?

1. Ron Cey
2. Steve Garvey
3. Pedro Guerrero
4. Mike Marshall
5. Mike Piazza
6. Reggie Smith

★ ◆ ★ ◆ ★

494. Who holds the Milwaukee Brewers career record for grand slams (5)?

1. Cecil Cooper
2. Paul Molitor
3. Ben Oglivie
4. George Scott
5. Gorman Thomas
6. Robin Yount

495. Who is the only pitcher in San Diego Padres history with two 20-win seasons?

1. Andy Benes
2. Pat Dobson
3. Randy Jones
4. Clay Kirby
5. Gaylord Perry
6. Eric Show

496. What season did the Angels finish with their first winning record?

1. 1962
2. 1964
3. 1967
4. 1970
5. 1978
6. 1979

497. Who holds the Montreal Expos career record for grand slams (7)?

1. Gary Carter
2. Andre Dawson
3. Ron Fairly
4. Al Oliver
5. Tim Raines
6. Tim Wallach

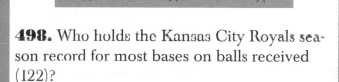

498. Who holds the Kansas City Royals season record for most bases on balls received (122)?

1. Willie Aikens
2. Steve Balboni
3. George Brett
4. Al Cowens
5. John Mayberry
6. Hal McRae

499. Who set the National League season record (150 games minimum) for highest fielding percentage for a shortstop (.987)?

1. Jay Bell
2. Larry Bowa
3. Rey Ordonez

500. How many managers have the New York Mets had?

1. 13
2. 15
3. 16
4. 19
5. 20
6. 22

501. What year did the St. Louis Cardinals win their first World Series?

1. 1926
2. 1931
3. 1935
4. 1942

502. How many managers have the Kansas City Royals had?

1. 9
2. 10
3. 13
4. 14
5. 16
6. 19

503. Who was the first man to hit a home run in 33 major league ballparks?

1. Hank Aaron
2. Ellis Burks
3. Mark McGwire
4. Frank Robinson

504. Who holds the National League career record for most games with four or more extra-base hits (4)?

1. Hank Aaron
2. Stan Hack
3. Ralph Kiner
4. Johnny Mize
5. Mike Schmidt
6. Willie Stargell

505. Which pitcher holds the American League career record for most home runs allowed (422)?

1. Bert Blyleven
2. Ned Garver
3. Red Ruffing
4. Frank Tanana

★ ◆ ★ ◆ ★

506. Who holds the American League season record for most chances accepted by an outfielder (524)?

1. Brady Anderson
2. Chet Lemon
3. Fred Lynn
4. Jim Piersall
5. Tris Speaker
6. Devon White

507. Who holds the American League record for most consecutive games scoring at least one run (18)?

1. Walt Dropo
2. Rickey Henderson
3. Red Rolfe
4. Willie Wilson

508. Who holds the Chicago White Sox season record for hits (222)?

1. Luis Aparicio
2. Luke Appling
3. Harold Baines
4. Eddie Collins
5. Nellie Fox
6. Joe Jackson
7. Robin Ventura

509. What's the furthest behind the league or division leader the Milwaukee Brewers ever finished?

1. 25½ games
2. 28 games
3. 32½ games
4. 35 games
5. 36½ games
6. 40 games

510. Who was the last Mariners pitcher to have a nine-game winning streak in one season?

1. Scott Bankhead
2. Dave Fleming
3. Randy Johnson
4. Mark Langston
5. Mike Moore
6. Bill Swift

511. Who holds the Colorado Rockies season record for most hits (211)?

1. Dante Bichette
2. Ellis Burks
3. Vinny Castilla
4. Andres Galarraga
5. Larry Walker
6. Eric Young

512. Who was the first pitcher to throw two shutouts in the same World Series?

1. Babe Adams
2. Chief Bender
3. Three-Finger Brown
4. Bill Dinneen
5. Christy Mathewson
6. George Mullin
7. Orval Overall

513. Who holds the Montreal Expos season record for most home runs hit (38)?

1. Gary Carter
2. Andre Dawson
3. Ron Fairly
4. Vladimir Guerrero
5. Al Oliver
6. Ken Singleton
7. Larry Walker

★ ◆ ★ ◆ ★

514. Which pitcher holds the Atlanta Braves season record for most strikeouts (276)?

1. Steve Avery
2. Tony Cloninger
3. Tom Glavine
4. Greg Maddux
5. John Smoltz
6. Warren Spahn

515. Which pitcher holds the major league career record for bases on balls allowed (2,795)?

1. Steve Carlton
2. Bob Feller
3. Charlie Hough
4. Phil Niekro
5. Nolan Ryan
6. Warren Spahn

★ ◆ ★ ◆ ★

516. Who was the first American League player to hit four home runs in a game?

1. Rocky Colavito
2. Jimmie Foxx
3. Lou Gehrig
4. Hank Greenberg
5. Babe Ruth
6. Kenny Williams

517. Which team holds the major league lead for most games leading their league or division at the end of the season (30)?

1. Atlanta Braves
2. Cleveland Indians
3. New York Yankees
4. Oakland Athletics

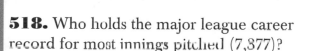

518. Who holds the major league career record for most innings pitched (7,377)?

1. Grover Cleveland Alexander
2. Walter Johnson
3. Christy Mathewson
4. Warren Spahn
5. Cy Young

519. Who holds the major league career record for highest batting average (.367)?

1. Ty Cobb
2. Eddie Collins
3. Rogers Hornsby
4. Napoleon Lajoie

520. Who holds the American League career record for most games played (3,308)?

1. Ty Cobb
2. Reggie Jackson
3. Cal Ripken, Jr.
4. Brooks Robinson
5. Ted Williams
6. Carl Yastrzemski

521. Which pitcher holds the American League season record for most shutouts lost (10)?

1. Jack Coombs
2. Walter Johnson
3. Ed Walsh
4. Doc White

522. When runs batted in became an official statistic in 1920, who set the first major league record for most RBI in a season (137)?

1. Happy Felsch
2. Rogers Hornsby
3. Joe Jackson
4. George Kelly
5. Babe Ruth
6. George Sisler

523. Who led the National League in home runs with 5 in 1876, the league's inaugural season?

1. Ross Barnes
2. George Hall
3. Paul Hines
4. George Shaffer

★　◆　★　◆　★

524. In 1901, the American League's first year as a major league, which player led the AL in batting average, runs, hits, singles, doubles, and home runs?

1. Ty Cobb
2. Harry Davis
3. Ed Delahanty
4. Dave Fultz
5. Napoleon Lajoie
6. Socks Seybold

525. Who holds the major league season record for highest batting average (.438)?

1. Ty Cobb
2. Hugh Duffy
3. Rogers Hornsby
4. Ducky Medwick
5. Babe Ruth
6. Ted Williams

526. Who holds the major league record for most consecutive games played from the start of his career (424)?

1. Ernie Banks
2. Harvey Kuenn
3. Tony Lazzeri
4. George Scott
5. Al Simmons
6. Billy Williams

527. Which team holds the American League season record for lowest batting average (.212)?

1. Chicago White Sox
2. New York Highlanders
3. Oakland A's
4. Philadelphia Athletics
5. Washington Senators

528. Which team holds the American League season record for most times grounding into a double play (174)?

1. Boston Red Sox
2. Cleveland Indians
3. Detroit Tigers
4. New York Yankees
5. St. Louis Browns
6. Washington Senators

529. Who was the first major leaguer to hit a grand slam (1881)?

1. Cap Anson
2. Roger Connor
3. Curry Foley
4. George Gore
5. Elmer Smith
6. Oscar Walker

530. When saves became an official statistic in 1969, who set the first major league record for most saves in a season (31)?

1. Fred Gladding
2. Wayne Granger
3. John Hiller
4. Sparky Lyle
5. Ron Perranoski
6. Ken Sanders

531. Which team holds the major league season record for home attendance (4,483,350)?

1. Atlanta Braves
2. Baltimore Orioles
3. Chicago White Sox
4. Cleveland Indians
5. Colorado Rockies
6. Los Angeles Dodgers

532. Who is the only major league pitcher to twice strike out eight consecutive batters in a game?

1. Roger Clemens
2. Ron Davis
3. Bob Feller
4. Randy Johnson
5. Pete Richert
6. Nolan Ryan

533. Who holds the San Francisco Giants' season record for highest batting average (.347)?

1. Barry Bonds
2. Will Clark
3. Willie Mays
4. Willie McCovey

★ ◆ ★ ◆ ★

534. Who holds the Atlanta Braves career record for most stolen bases (174)?

1. Ron Gant
2. Ralph Garr
3. Dale Murphy
4. Otis Nixon
5. Jerry Royster
6. Michael Tucker

535. Who holds the Toronto Blue Jays season record for most stolen bases (60)?

1. Roberto Alomar
2. Dave Collins
3. Alfredo Griffin
4. Devon White

536. Before John Wetteland broke the team record in 1998 with 42 saves, who held the Texas Rangers season record for saves with 40?

1. Tom Henke
2. Mike Henneman
3. Jim Kern
4. Jeff Russell
5. Dave Schmidt
6. Mitch Williams

537. What year did the San Diego Padres first finish with a winning record?

1. 1978
2. 1980
3. 1982
4. 1984

538. In their 21 years of existence, how many seasons have the Seattle Mariners finished with a winning record?

1. 2
2. 4
3. 5
4. 6
5. 8
6. 9

539. What is the lowest season winning percentage in New York Yankees history?

1. .329
2. .331
3. .414
4. .421

540. Which pitcher holds the Minnesota Twins season record for complete games (25)?

1. Bert Blyleven
2. Scott Erickson
3. Jim Kaat
4. Jim Perry
5. Brad Radke
6. Kevin Tapani
7. Frank Viola

541. Mark McGwire's 70 homers in 1998 broke whose St. Louis Cardinals single-season record of 43?

1. Pedro Guerrero
2. Rogers Hornsby
3. Johnny Mize
4. Stan Musial

542. Before divisional play, what was the American League record for most games ahead at the end of the season for a pennant winner?

1. 17
2. 19
3. 19½
4. 20½
5. 22
6. 30

543. Who holds the Milwaukee Brewers season record for triples (16)?

1. Jim Gantner
2. Tommy Harper
3. Larry Hisle
4. Pat Listach
5. Paul Molitor
6. Robin Yount

544. Who holds the Pittsburgh Pirates career record for total bases (4,492)?

1. Roberto Clemente
2. Charlie Grimm
3. Ralph Kiner
4. Willie Stargell
5. Honus Wagner
6. Paul Waner

545. What was the first season the Kansas City Royals finished with a winning record?

1. 1971
2. 1973
3. 1975
4. 1976
5. 1977
6. 1978

546. Which pitcher holds the New York Mets season record for most 1–0 shutouts won (3)?

1. David Cone
2. Roger Craig
3. Dwight Gooden
4. Jerry Koosman
5. Bob Ojeda
6. Tom Seaver

547. Who has the longest batting streak in Cleveland Indians history (31 games)?

1. Earl Averill
2. Larry Doby
3. Napoleon Lajoie
4. Kenny Lofton
5. Tris Speaker
6. Leon Wagner

548. Who holds the Montreal Expos season record for most bases on balls received (123)?

1. Hubie Brooks
2. Gary Carter
3. Andre Dawson
4. Ron Fairly
5. Ron Hunt
6. Tim Raines
7. Ken Singleton

549. What season did the Chicago White Sox finish with their highest winning percentage (.649)?

1. 1906
2. 1917
3. 1919
4. 1959
5. 1983
6. 1994

550. Who holds the Houston Astros season record for highest batting average (.333)?

1. Jeff Bagwell
2. Craig Biggio
3. Cesar Cedeno
4. Jose Cruz
5. Joe Morgan
6. Rusty Staub

551. Which team holds the major league record for most grand slams hit in one season (12)?

1. Atlanta Braves
2. Pittsburgh Pirates
3. San Francisco Giants
4. Seattle Mariners

552. Which team's pitching staff holds the major league record for most balks in one season (76)?

1. Colorado Rockies
2. Cleveland Indians
3. Milwaukee Brewers
4. Oakland A's
5. Seattle Pilots
6. Washington Senators

553. Who holds the National League season record for most at-bats by a switch-hitter (695)?

1. Howard Johnson
2. Pete Rose
3. Quilvio Veras
4. Maury Wills

554. Who holds the major league season record for most at-bats by a pinch hitter (81)?

1. Gates Brown
2. Jim Dwyer
3. Manny Mota
4. Dusty Rhodes
5. Rusty Staub
6. John Vander Wal

555. Who holds the American League record for longest hitting streak from the start of the season (34 games)?

1. Joe DiMaggio
2. Ron LeFlore
3. Paul Molitor
4. George Sisler

556. Who holds the major league record for most consecutive years played (26)?

1. Ty Cobb
2. Eddie Collins
3. Stan Musial
4. Pete Rose
5. Nolan Ryan
6. Carl Yastrzemski

557. What is the most players used in one season by a major league team?

1. 48
2. 53
3. 54
4. 56

558. What is the fewest players used in one season (162 games) by a major league team?

1. 27
2. 28
3. 29
4. 30
5. 31
6. 32
7. 33

559. Who is the only major leaguer to play 150 or more games in 13 consecutive seasons?

1. Steve Garvey
2. Lou Gehrig
3. Willie Mays
4. Cal Ripken, Jr.
5. Pete Rose
6. Carl Yastrzemski

560. Who was the last major leaguer to hit two inside-the-park home runs in one game?

1. Phil Bradley
2. Vince Coleman
3. Greg Gagne
4. Ralph Garr
5. Willie Kirkland
6. Karl Rhodes
7. Hank Thompson

561. Who holds the American League career record for total bases (5,862)?

1. Ty Cobb
2. Mickey Mantle
3. Jim Rice
4. Babe Ruth
5. Ted Williams
6. Carl Yastrzemski

562. Who holds the American League career record for most putouts by a first baseman (19,754)?

1. Lou Gehrig
2. Joe Judge
3. Don Mattingly
4. Stuffy McInnis
5. Vic Power
6. Mickey Vernon

563. Which pitcher holds the major league season record for most consecutive games lost (19)?

1. Roger Craig
2. Cliff Curtis
3. Jack Nabors
4. Bobo Newsome
5. Anthony Young

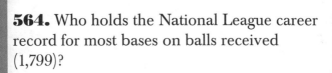

564. Who holds the National League career record for most bases on balls received (1,799)?

1. Hank Aaron
2. Willie McCovey
3. Joe Morgan
4. Mel Ott
5. Mike Schmidt
6. Jim Wynn

565. Who is the only American League player to reach base on errors three times in one game?

1. Earl Averill
2. Dale Berra
3. Phil Bradley
4. Dan Meyer
5. Sam Rice

566. Who was the last player to go an entire season (150 or more games played) without grounding into a double play?

1. Craig Biggio
2. Vince Coleman
3. Augie Galan
4. Kenny Lofton
5. Mookie Wilson
6. Willie Wilson

567. Which team holds the major league record for the highest season batting average since 1900 (.319)?

1. Boston Red Sox
2. Chicago Cubs
3. Detroit Tigers
4. New York Giants
5. New York Yankees
7. St. Louis Cardinals

★ ◆ ★ ◆ ★

568. Who was the first major leaguer to drive in 13 runs in a doubleheader?

1. Ernie Banks
2. Jim Bottomley
3. Nate Colbert
4. Carl Furillo
5. Mark Whiten
6. Hack Wilson

569. Who holds the National League record for most consecutive games played with no caught stealing (592)?

1. Sandy Amoros
2. Ron Cey
3. Frank Torre
4. Maury Wills

★ ◆ ★ ◆ ★

570. Who holds the National League career record for most double plays by an outfielder (86)?

1. Jesse Barfield
2. Barry Bonds
3. Max Carey
4. Ken Griffey, Sr.
5. Willie Mays
6. Joe Medwick

571. Who holds the St. Louis Browns season record for singles (179)?

1. Beau Bell
2. George Sisler
3. Jack Tobin
4. Ken Williams

572. Who holds the American League career record for most assists by a first baseman (1,444)?

1. Jimmie Foxx
2. Lou Gehrig
3. Don Mattingly
4. Eddie Murray
5. Vic Power
6. Mickey Vernon

573. Which pitcher holds the major league rookie season record for most shutouts won or tied (16)?

1. George Bradley
2. Russ Ford
3. Bob Grim
4. Fernando Valenzuela

574. Who holds the Baltimore Orioles season record for total bases (369)?

1. Brady Anderson
2. Mike Devereaux
3. Jim Gentile
4. Eddie Murray
5. Cal Ripken
6. Ken Singleton

575. Who holds the Los Angeles Dodgers season record for doubles (47)?

1. Ron Cey
2. Steve Garvey
3. Wes Parker
4. Reggie Smith

576. Who holds the major league record for most games pitched by a rookie (83)?

1. Elroy Face
2. Mike Marshall
3. Mike Myers
4. Gregg Olson
5. Kent Tekulve
6. Bobby Thigpen
7. Todd Worrell

577. Who holds the Chicago White Sox career record for doubles (440)?

1. Luke Appling
2. Eddie Collins
3. Nellie Fox
4. Joe Jackson
5. Frank Thomas
6. Greg Walker

578. Who holds the Florida Marlins career record for total bases (1,181)?

1. Bobby Bonilla
2. Chuck Carr
3. Jeff Conine
4. Cliff Floyd
5 Edgar Renteria
6. Gary Sheffield
7. Walt Weiss

579. Who holds the major league record for most consecutive years leading his league in fielding percentage as a catcher (6)?

1. Bob Boone
2. Gary Carter
3. Carlton Fisk
4. Bill Freehan
5. Tom Haller
6. Jim Sundberg

★ ◆ ★ ◆ ★

580. Who holds the Minnesota Twins career record for total bases (3,453)?

1. Tom Brunansky
2. Gary Gaetti
3. Harmon Killebrew
4. Tony Oliva
5. Vic Power
6. Kirby Puckett

581. Who holds the New York Giants season record for singles (177)?

1. Larry Doyle
2. Frankie Frisch
3. Rogers Hornsby
4. George Kelly
5. Willie Mays
6. Bill Terry

582. Who holds the post-1900 National League career record for hit batsmen (154)?

1. Grover Alexander
2. Dizzy Dean
3. Don Drysdale
4. Bob Gibson
5. Sandy Koufax
6. Eppa Rixey
7. Nolan Ryan

583. Who holds the Detroit Tigers season record for most times being hit by a pitch (24)?

1. Ty Cobb
2. Mickey Cochrane
3. Sam Crawford
4. Bill Freehan
5. Charlie Gehringer
6. Willie Horton

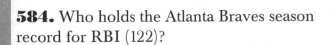

584. Who holds the Atlanta Braves season record for RBI (122)?

1. Hank Aaron
2. Bob Horner
3. Davey Johnson
4. Eddie Mathews
5. Dale Murphy
6. Jimmy Wynn

585. What's the record for most stolen bases by both teams in a game?

1. 16
2. 18
3. 19
4. 21
5. 22
6. 23

586. Who was the only man to pitch to both Babe Ruth and Mickey Mantle in major league games?

1. Al Benton
2. Bob Feller
3. Wes Ferrell
4. Lefty Grove
5. Hal Newhouser
6. Bobo Newsom

587. When Willie Mays hit his 600th home run, who was he pinch-hitting for?

1. George Foster
2. Jim Ray Hart
3. Willie McCovey
4. Hank Thompson

588. Who is the only batter to lead his league in hits his first three major league seasons?

1. Ty Cobb
2. Carney Lansford
3. Bill Madlock
4. Tony Oliva
5. Mel Ott
6. Johnny Pesky

589. Who is the only batter in major league history to hit 50 or more home runs in a season while striking out less than 50 times?

1. Rogers Hornsby
2. Johnny Mize
3. Stan Musial
4. Ted Williams

590. Who was the last batter to homer for the Brooklyn Dodgers?

1. Sandy Amoros
2. Gil Hodges
3. Ransom Jackson
4. Wally Moon
5. Don Newcombe
6. Don Zimmer

591. Who is the only major leaguer to bat .400 and hit 40 home runs in the same season?

1. Rogers Hornsby
2. Babe Ruth
3. George Sisler
4. Ted Williams

★ ◆ ★ ◆ ★

592. Which pitcher gave up Hank Aaron's 714th home run?

1. Jack Billingham
2. Pedro Borbon
3. Larry Dierker
4. Al Downing
5. Don Gullett
6. Phil Niekro
7. Fred Norman

593. Who hit the first official grand slam ever to be hit in interleague play?

1. Rich Aurilia
2. Jim Eisenreich
3. Matt Franco
4. Fred McGriff
5. Sammy Sosa
6. Todd Zeile

★　◆　★　◆　★

594. Who was the only player on a New York team to homer in both Shea Stadium and Yankee Stadium in 1997?

1. Carlos Baerga
2. Bernard Gilkey
3. Todd Hundley
4. Tino Martinez
5. Tim Raines
6. Luis Sojo

595. Who was the losing pitcher in the only nine-inning complete game in which there was only one hit?

1. Steve Carlton
2. Joe Cowley
3. Andy Hawkins
4. Bob Hendley
5. Frank Tanana

596. Who holds the record for most years active in the major leagues without being on a pennant-winning team (25)?

1. Ernie Banks
2. Roger Craig
3. Rabbit Maranville
4. Bill Virdon
5. Bobby Wallace
6. Ted Williams

597. Who drove in the winning run for the New York Mets on April 7, 1970, the first time in team history it won on Opening Day?

1. Tommie Agee
2. Donn Clendenon
3. Cleon Jones
4. Bobby Pfeil
5. Ron Swoboda

598. Which pitcher holds the major league record for most appearances without a loss from the start of his career?

1. Grover Cleveland Alexander
2. Mike DeJean
3. Al Hrabosky
4. Phil Paine
5. Nolan Ryan
6. Hoyt Wilhelm

599. Who holds the major league record for most total bases in a single game as a leadoff hitter (15)?

1. Bobby Bonds
2. Dom DiMaggio
3. Rickey Henderson
4. Kenny Lofton
5. Davey Lopes
6. Tim Raines

600. Who was the last player to steal home to win a 1–0 game?

1. Rod Carew
2. Ty Cobb
3. Kenny Lofton
4. Omar Moreno
5. Jim Thome
6. Mark Whiten

601. Who is the only pitcher to end a World Series with a wild pitch?

1. Ray Kremer
2. Dave McNally
3. John Miljus
4. Bob Stanley

602. Who was the winning pitcher in the fastest major league game on record (51 minutes)?

1. Grover Alexander
2. Jesse Barnes
3. Mordecai Brown
4. Jack Chesbro
5. Walter Johnson
6. Dutch Leonard
7. Christy Mathewson

603. Who was the winning pitcher in the first All-Star game?

1. General Crowder
2. Lefty Gomez
3. Lefty Grove
4. Carl Hubbell

604. Who was the first batter in the first All-Star game?

1. Jimmie Dykes
2. Frankie Frisch
3. Chuck Klein
4. Pepper Martin
5. Joe Sewell
6. Arkie Vaughn
7. Paul Waner

605. Who hit the Tampa Bay Devil Rays' first inside-the-park home run?

1. Roberto Kelly
2. Aaron Ledesma
3. Dave Martinez
4. Quinton McCracken

606. What was the first National League team to reach the million mark in attendance?

1. Cincinnati Reds
2. Chicago Cubs
3. Los Angeles Dodgers
4. New York Giants
5. New York Mets
6. San Francisco Giants
7. St. Louis Cardinals

607. Who was the first player to homer in his first World Series at-bat?

1. Jack Graney
2. Joe Harris
3. Babe Ruth
4. Gene Tenace

608. Who committed the first error in an All-Star game?

1. Dick Bartell
2. Lou Gehrig
3. Babe Herman
4. Carl Hubbell
5. Chuck Klein
6. Al Simmons

609. Who was the first black pitcher to throw a no-hitter in the major leagues?

1. Vida Blue
2. Bob Gibson
3. Sam Jones
4. Don Newcombe

610. What was the first National League team to reach two million in season attendance?

1. Chicago Cubs
2. Houston Astros
3. Los Angeles Dodgers
4. Milwaukee Braves
5. New York Mcts
6. San Francisco Giants
7. St. Louis Cardinals

611. Who hit the first major league grand slam in Canada?

1. Rico Carty
2. Mack Jones
3. Coco Laboy
4. Dal Maxvill
5. Mike Shannon
6. Gary Waslewski

612. Who hit the first All-Star pinch-hit homer?

1. Jim Bottomley
2. Mickey Cochrane
3. Bill Dickey
4. Mickey Owen
5. Riggs Stephenson
6. Bill Terry

613. Who was the first man to bat for the American League in an All-Star game?

1. Ossie Bluege
2. Ben Chapman
3. Joe Cronin
4. Frank Crosetti
5. Billy Rogell
6. Joe Sewell

614. Who was the first man to bat in a major league night game?

1. Lou Chiozza
2. Rip Collins
3. Stan Hack
4. Pee Wee Reese
5. Pete Reiser
6. Dixie Walker

615. Who was the first player to hit two home runs in a single All-Star game?

1. Augie Galan
2. Goose Goslin
3. Heinie Manush
4. Joe Medwick
5. Arky Vaughan
6. Ted Williams

616. Who was the winning pitcher in the first major league game played on artificial turf?

1. Don Cardwell
2. Mike Cuellar
3. Joey Jay
4. Ray Sadecki
5. Don Sutton
6. Bob Veale

617. Who surrendered Hank Aaron's first major league home run?

1. Ralph Branca
2. Jim Hearn
3. Dave Koslo
4. Lindy McDaniel
5. Gaylord Perry
6. Vic Raschi

618. Who was the first player to steal home in a World Series game?

1. Ty Cobb
2. Bill Dahlen
3. Tommy Leach
4. Bris Lord
5. Babe Ruth
6. Honus Wagner

619. Who holds the major league record for home runs by a rookie (49)?

1. Dave Kingman
2. Mark McGwire
3. Babe Ruth
4. Rudy York

620. Who holds the National League record for most seasons leading the league in fielding percentage?

1. Carl Furillo
2. Steve Garvey
3. Junior Gilliam
4. Rabbit Maranville
5. Joe Morgan
6. Ozzie Smith

621. Who holds the Texas Rangers record for home runs by a rookie (30)?

1. Jeff Burroughs
2. Juan Gonzalez
3. Pete Incaviglia
4. Ruben Sierra

622. Who holds the major league season record for grand slams (6)?

1. Ernie Banks
2. Rocky Colavito
3. Lou Gehrig
4. Don Mattingly
5. Frank Thomas
6. Hack Wilson

623. Who holds the American League record for most years leading the league in putouts by a first baseman (4)?

1. Jiggs Donahue
2. Wally Pipp
3. Vic Power
4. Mickey Vernon

624. Which franchise holds the major league record for most consecutive seasons hitting 100 or more home runs (35)?

1. Boston Red Sox
2. Chicago Cubs
3. Cincinnati Reds
4. Detroit Tigers
5. New York Giants
6. New York Yankees

625. Who holds the Baltimore Orioles season record for RBI (142)?

1. Lee May
2. Rafael Palmeiro
3. Boog Powell
4. Ken Singleton

626. Which team holds the American League record for most consecutive years without winning a league championship (42)?

1. Boston Red Sox
2. Chicago White Sox
3. Cleveland Indians
4. Kansas City Athletics
5. St. Louis Browns
6. Washington Senators

627. Who holds the National League season record for highest slugging percentage by a lefthanded batter in a minimum of 100 games (.720)?

1. Willie McCovey
2. Johnny Mize
3. Bill Terry
4. Larry Walker

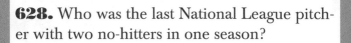

628. Who was the last National League pitcher with two no-hitters in one season?

1. Grover Alexander
2. Steve Carlton
3. Sandy Koufax
4. Jim Maloney
5. Nolan Ryan
6. Johnny Vander Meer

629. Who holds the San Diego Padres season record for extra-base hits (84)?

1. Ken Caminiti
2. Jack Clark
3. Nate Colbert
4. Steve Finley
5. Steve Garvey
6. Tony Gwynn

630. Who holds the Atlanta Braves season record for slugging percentage (.669)?

1. Hank Aaron
2. Darrell Evans
3. Bob Horner
4. Dave Johnson
5. Eddie Mathews
6. Dale Murphy

631. Which pitcher holds the major league record for most seasons leading his league in hit batsmen (6)?

1. Don Drysdale
2. Howard Ehmke
3. Bob Gibson
4. Walter Johnson
5. Joe McGinnity
6. Wilbur Wood

★ ◆ ★ ◆ ★

632. Who holds the major league record for consecutive games played by a catcher (312)?

1. Bob Boone
2. Jack Clements
3. Frankie Hayes
4. Randy Hundley
5. Al Lopez
6. Jim Sundberg

633. Which pitcher is the Chicago Cubs career leader in shutouts (48)?

1. Grover Alexander
2. Mordecai Brown
3. John Clarkson
4. Dizzy Dean
5. Orval Overall
6. Rick Sutcliffe

634. Who led the American League in batting average in 1961?

1. Norm Cash
2. Jackie Jensen
3. Mickey Mantle
4. Roger Maris
5. Minnie Minoso
6. Jimmy Piersall

635. Who was the last Montreal Expo to play 162 games in a season?

1. Gary Carter
2. Warren Cromartie
3. Mark Grudzielanek
4. Tim Raines
5. Ken Singleton
6. Tim Wallach

636. What year did Babe Ruth set the major league record of 119 extra-base hits in one season?

1. 1920
2. 1921
3. 1923
4. 1925
5. 1927
6. 1928

637. Who holds the Philadelphia Phillies season record for grand slams (4)?

1. Vince DiMaggio
2. Chuck Klein
3. Lefty O'Doul
4. Mike Schmidt

638. Who holds the New York Yankees career record for RBI (1,990)?

1. Yogi Berra
2. Earl Coombs
3. Joe DiMaggio
4. Lou Gehrig
5. Mickey Mantle
6. Babe Ruth

639. Who holds the Los Angeles Dodgers career record for at-bats (7,495)?

1. Ron Cey
2. Willie Davis
3. Bill Russell
4. Maury Wills

640. Who holds the National League record for most total bases by a rookie (352)?

1. Joe Adcock
2. Richie Allen
3. Johnny Bench
4. Johnny Frederick
5. Chuck Klein
6. Frank Robinson

641. Who holds the major league season record for balks (16)?

1. Bert Blyleven
2. Steve Carlton
3. Vic Raschi
4. Dave Stewart

642. Who was the last major league shortstop to make five errors in one game?

1. Donie Bush
2. Bucky Dent
3. Shawon Dunston
4. Johnny Gochnaur
5. Dick Groat
6. Zoilo Versalles

643. Who was the first major leaguer to hit two grand slams in one game?

1. Lou Gehrig
2. Tony Lazzeri
3. Babe Ruth
4. Rudy York

644. Which pitcher holds the major league career record for runs allowed (2,117)?

1. Lefty Gomez
2. Bobo Newsom
3. Red Ruffing
4. Nolan Ryan
5. Early Wynn
6. Cy Young

645. Which pitcher holds the Montreal Expos season record for losses (22)?

1. Bill Gullickson
2. Carl Morton
3. Pascual Perez
4. Steve Renko
5. Steve Rogers
6. Bill Stoneman

646. Which pitcher holds the Chicago White Sox season record for strikeouts (269)?

1. Ed Cicotte
2. Jack Harshman
3. LaMarr Hoyt
4. Ted Lyons
5. Ed A. Walsh
6. Wilbur Wood

647. Who holds the New York Giants career record for stolen bases (334)?

1. George J. Burns
2. George Davis
3. Larry Doyle
4. Willie Mays
5. Fred Merkle
6. Joe Moore

648. Who holds the Cleveland Indians season record for RBI (162)?

1. Albert Belle
2. Larry Doby
3. Al Rosen
4. Tris Speaker
5. Hal Trosky
6. Vic Wertz

649. Who was the first manager to win an AL pennant with the Oakland A's?

1. Hank Bauer
2. Alvin Dark
3. Bob Kennedy
4. John McNamara
5. Chuck Tanner
6. Dick Williams

★ ◆ ★ ◆ ★

650. Who holds the Pittsburgh Pirates season record for doubles (62)?

1. Roberto Clemente
2. Ralph Kiner
3. Bob Robertson
4. Willie Stargell
5. Paul Waner
6. Owen Wilson

651. Who is the Mets career leader in at-bats (5,436)?

1. Tommie Agee
2. Hubie Brooks
3. Todd Hundley
4. Cleon Jones
5. Ed Kranepool
6. Mookie Wilson

652. Who holds the Kansas City Royals season record for home runs (36)?

1. Steve Balboni
2. George Brett
3. Chili Davis
4. Bob Hamelin
5. Hal McRae
6. Amos Otis

653. Who holds the Houston Astros season record for runs scored (146)?

1. Jeff Bagwell
2. Craig Biggio
3. Cesar Cedeno
4. Jose Cruz
5. Joe Morgan
6. Rusty Staub

654. Who holds the Philadelphia Phillies season record for hits (254)?

1. Richie Ashburn
2. Ed Delahanty
3. Von Hayes
4. Mickey Morandini
5. Lefty O'Doul
6. Pete Rose

655. Who holds the American League career record for wild pitches (206)?

1. Joaquin Andujar
2. Randy Johnson
3. Walter Johnson
4. Jack Morris

656. Who holds the St. Louis Cardinals season record for games played (163)?

1. Lou Brock
2. Taylor Douthit
3. Frankie Frisch
4. Ray Lankford
5. Jose Oquendo
6. Ozzie Smith

657. Who holds the major league rookie record for bases on balls received (107)?

1. Jack Clark
2. Nomar Garciaparra
3. Frank Thomas
4. Ted Williams

658. Who holds the Oakland A's record for most consecutive games driving in a run (10)?

1. Bert Campaneris
2. Reggie Jackson
3. Rick Monday
4. Dwayne Murphy
5. Joe Rudi
6. Gene Tenace

659. Who holds the major league record for most years leading his league in assists by a pitcher (6)?

1. Jack Chesbro
2. Jim Kaat
3. Bob Lemon
4. Ed Walsh

660. Before Mark McGwire hit 70 in 1998, who held the St. Louis Cardinals season record for most home runs by a righthanded batter (42)?

1. Dick Allen
2. Ken Boyer
3. Jack Clark
4. George Hendrick
5. Rogers Hornsby
6. Stan Musial

661. When was the last time two teams played four consecutive extra-inning games?

1. 1912
2. 1943
3. 1956
4. 1968

662. Who holds the Detroit Tigers season record for highest slugging percentage (.683)?

1. Norm Cash
2. Rocky Colavito
3. Cecil Fielder
4. Charlie Gehringer
5. Hank Greenberg
6. Al Kaline
7. Rudy York

663. Who holds the American League record for most years leading outfielders in chances accepted (8)?

1. Paul Blair
2. Ty Cobb
3. Joe DiMaggio
4. Jim Northrup
5. Tris Speaker
6. Robin Yount

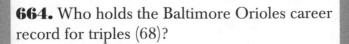

664. Who holds the Baltimore Orioles career record for triples (68)?

1. Brady Anderson
2. Luis Aparicio
3. Paul Blair
4. Cal Ripken, Jr.
5. Brooks Robinson
6. Ken Singleton

665. Who holds the American League record for most doubles allowed in one inning (6)?

1. Mike Caldwell
2. Lefty Grove
3. Walter Johnson
4. Fred Marberry
5. Jim Perry
6. Al Travers

666. Who was the first Toronto Blue Jay to hit a pinch home run in his first major league at-bat?

1. Rick Bosetti
2. Kelly Gruber
3. Fred McGriff
4. Lloyd Moseby
5. Ed Sprague
6. Al Woods

667. Who holds the major league record for most runners left on base in one game (12)?

1. Glenn Beckert
2. Mark Belanger
3. Frank Isbell
4. John Milner
5. Ozzie Smith
6. Joe Torre

668. Who holds the Texas Rangers record for most home runs in a month (15)?

1. Jeff Burroughs
2. Juan Gonzalez
3. Pete Incaviglia
4. Rafael Palmeiro
5. Dean Palmer
6. Ruben Sierra

669. Which team holds the National League season record for most double plays (215)?

1. Atlanta Braves
2. Chicago Cubs
3. Los Angeles Dodgers
4. New York Giants
5. Pittsburgh Pirates
6. St. Louis Cardinals

670. Which pitcher holds the Houston Astros season record for most victories (21)?

1 Larry Dierker
2. Darryl Kile
3. Joe Niekro
4. J.R. Richards
5. Nolan Ryan
6. Mike Scott

671. Who is the last American League player with 7 stolen bases in two consecutive games?

1. Ty Cobb
2. Rickey Henderson
3. Ron LeFlore
4. Kenny Lofton
5. Amos Otis
6. Willie Wilson

672. Who holds the San Francisco Giants career record for most home runs (469)?

1. Barry Bonds
2. Bobby Bonds
3. Will Clark
4. Jim Ray Hart
5. Willie Mays
6. Willie McCovey

673. Who holds the Minnesota Twins season record for most home runs by a lefthanded batter (34)?

1. Jimmie Hall
2. Kent Hrbek
3. Harmon Killebrew
4. Tony Oliva

674. Who holds the Florida Marlins season record for most doubles (45)?

1. Moises Alou
2. Bobby Bonilla
3. Jeff Conine
4. Cliff Floyd
5. Gary Sheffield
6. Devon White

675. Which pitcher holds the Milwaukee Brewers season record for most hit batters (16)?

1. Pete Broberg
2. Ted Higuera
3. Jeff Juden
4. Jim Slaton

676. Who holds the Houston Astros record for most home runs by a rookie (20)?

1. Jeff Bagwell
2. Kevin Bass
3. Derek Bell
4. Jose Cruz
5. Glenn Davis
6. Jimmy Wynn

677. Who holds the Baltimore Orioles season record for most extra-base hits (92)?

1. Brady Anderson
2. Eddie Murray
3. Boog Powell
4. Brooks Robinson

678. Who holds the Kansas City Royals season record for most times caught stealing (22)?

1. Buddy Biancalala
2. Johnny Damon
3. Tom Goodwin
4. Freddie Patek
5. Frank White
6. Willie Wilson

679. Who holds the Philadelphia Phillies career record for most runs scored (1,506)?

1. Richie Ashburn
2. Chuck Klein
3. Pete Rose
4. Mike Schmidt

680. Prior to divisional play, who managed the Detroit Tigers to their widest pennant-winning margin (12 games)?

1. Del Baker
2. Ty Cobb
3. Mickey Cochrane
4. Hughey Jennings
5. Steve O'Neill
6. Bob Scheffing
7. Mayo Smith

681. Which pitcher holds the Boston Red Sox season record for home runs allowed (38)?

1. Howard Ehmke
2. Tex Hughson
3. Mel Parnell
4. Red Ruffing
5. Jack Russell
6. Tim Wakefield

682. Who holds the St. Louis Cardinals career record for home runs by a right-handed batter (255)?

1. Ken Boyer
2. Keith Hermandez
3. Joe Mcdwick
4. Stan Musial
5. Ted Simmons
6. Joe Torre

683. Who holds the Chicago White Sox career record for most singles (2,162)?

1. Luke Appling
2. Harold Baines
3. Eddie Collins
4. Nellie Fox
5. Joe Jackson
6. Minnie Minoso

684. Who holds the Cincinnati Reds season record for triples (25)?

1. Sam Crawford
2. Eric Davis
3. Arlie Latham
4. Bid McPhee
5. Joe Morgan
6. Pete Rose
7. Ed Roush

685. Who was the last Angel to play 162 games in a season?

1. Sandy Alomar
2. Don Baylor
3. Brian Downing
4. Jim Edmonds
5. Tim Foli
6. Johnny Ray

686. Which pitcher holds the Los Angeles Dodgers season record for most bases on balls allowed (124)?

1. Sandy Koufax
2. Ramon Martinez
3. Hideo Nomo
4. Claude Osteen
5. Don Sutton
6. Fernando Valenzuela

687. Who managed the Cleveland Indians to their first pennant?

1. Bill Armour
2. Lou Boudreau
3. Lee Fohl
4. Napoleon Lajoie
5. Al Lopez
6. Tris Speaker

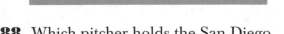

688. Which pitcher holds the San Diego Padres career record for most victories (100)?

1. Andy Benes
2. Dave Dravecky
3. Andy Hawkins
4. Randy Jones
5. Fred Norman
6. Eric Show

689. Who holds the season record for highest road attendance (2,944,157)?

1. Atlanta Braves
2. Cleveland Indians
3. New York Yankees
4. Seattle Mariners

690. Who holds the National League season record for most balks (11)?

1. Joaquin Andujar
2. Steve Carlton
3. Bruce Hurst
4. Pedro Martinez
5. Hideo Nomo
6. Donovan Osborne

691. Who holds the major league record for most sacrifices (511)?

1. Eddie Collins
2. Jake Daubert
3. Tommy Herr
4. Bill Mazeroski

692. Who was the last player to have 9 hits in a doubleheader?

1. Harvey Kuenn
2. Hal McRay
3. Danny Tartabull
4. Lee Thomas
5. Pete Runnels
6. Vic Wertz
7. Alan Wiggins

693. Who holds the American League record for most consecutive stolen bases with no caught stealing (40)?

1. Eric Davis
2. Kenny Lofton
3. Tim Raines
4. Willie Wilson

694. Which pitcher holds the American League season record for most wins by a left-hander (31)?

1. Lefty Gomez
2. Lefty Grove
3. Denny McLain
4. Dave McNally
5. Hal Newhouser
6. Babe Ruth

695. Who holds the major league season record for most bases on balls allowed (276)?

1. Bob Feller
2. Sam Jones
3. Amos Rusie
4. Nolan Ryan

696. Who holds the major league record for most assists in a extra-inning game by a second baseman (15)?

1. Lave Cross
2. Jim Gilliam
3. Glenn Hubbard
4. Don Money
5. Morrie Rath
6. Bobby Richardson
7. Ryne Sandberg

697. Who is the only major league player who has hit four home runs in one game as a batter and (in a separate game) struck out the side in an inning of pitching?

1. Rocky Colavito
2. Stan Musial
3. Babe Ruth
4. Mark Whiten

698. Who holds the major league season record for most pinch-hitting appearances (94)?

1. Gates Brown
2. Jerry Lynch
3. Manny Mota
4. Rusty Staub
5. Elmer Valo
6. John Vander Wal

699. Who is the only major leaguer to lead his league in at-bats seven times?

1. Doc Cramer
2. Abner Dalrymple
3. Cal Ripken
4. Pete Rose
5. Maury Wills
6. Willie Wilson

700. Who holds the National League rookie record for most times hit-by-pitch (20)?

1. Jay Bell
2. Hugh Critz
3. Granny Hamner
4. Ron Hunt
5. Frank Robinson
6. F.P. Santangelo

701. Which pitcher holds the major league career record for most games won from one club (70)?

1. Grover Alexander
2. Bob Gibson
3. Lefty Grove
4. Walter Johnson
5. Juan Marichal
7. Cy Young

702. What year did Connie Mack win his first major league pennant as manager?

1. 1895
2. 1901
3. 1902
4. 1903
5. 1904
6. 1910

703. When was the last year hitters playing in the same city led the American League and the National League in batting average?

1. 1906
2. 1920
3. 1922
4. 1942
5. 1949
6. 1953

704. Who is the last pitcher to start four double plays in a game?

1. Wilbur Cooper
2. Willis Hudlin
3. Jim Kaat
4. Hal Newhouser
5. Clay Parker
6. Warren Spahn

705. Who holds the Baltimore Orioles career record for most hits?

1. Eddie Murray
2. Cal Ripken, Jr.
3. Brooks Robinson
4. Frank Robinson

706. Who was the first man to win three American League batting average championships?

1. Ty Cobb
2. Ed Delahanty
3. Joe Jackson
4. Napoleon Lajoie
5. Al Simmons
6. George Sisler
7. Tris Speaker

707. Who was the first man to win six straight American League slugging average championships?

1. Frank Baker
2. Ty Cobb
3. Jimmie Foxx
4. Babe Ruth

★ ◆ ★ ◆ ★

708. Among active major league players, who has the most 200-hit seasons?

1. Wade Boggs
2. Tony Gwynn
3. John Olerud
4. Cal Ripken, Jr.
5. Frank Thomas
6. Larry Walker

709. How many men have played 1,000 or more consecutive major league games?

   1. 4
   2. 5
   3. 6
   4. 7

710. Before the 1998 season, who was the last player to hit more than 50 home runs in a National League season?

   1. Andre Dawson
   2. George Foster
   3. Dave Kingman
   4. Willie Mays
   5. Willie McCovey
   4. Mike Schmidt

711. Who was the first Mets reliever to lead the National League in saves?

1. John Franco
2. Skip Lockwood
3. Roger McDowell
4. Tug McGraw
5. Randy Myers
6. Jesse Orosco

712. Who was the first player to lead the American League in stolen bases in two seasons?

1. Harry Bay
2. Ty Cobb
3. Eddie Collins
4. Elmer Flick
5. Frank Isbell
6. Napoleon Lajoie

713. Which was the first National League team to be shut out?

1. Boston
2. Buffalo
3. Chicago
4. Cincinnati
5. Louisville
6. Philadelphia

714. Who holds the major league career record for most chances accepted by a catcher?

1. Yogi Berra
2. Bob Boone
3. Gary Carter
4. Carlton Fisk
5. Al Lopez
6. Jim Sundberg

715. Which pitcher holds the American League career record for most losses by a left-hander?

1. Bob Feller
2. Lefty Gomez
3. Lefty Grove
4. Walter Johnson
5. Eddie Plank
6. Frank Tanana

716. Who is the only player to have 150 or more RBI in 7 major league seasons?

1. Jimmie Foxx
2. Lou Gehrig
3. Hank Greenberg
4. Rogers Hornsby
5. Babe Ruth
6. Ted Williams

717. Which team holds the American League season record for most hits?

1. Boston Red Sox
2. Cleveland Indians
3. Detroit Tigers
4. Minnesota Twins
5. New York Yankees
6. Toronto Blue Jays

718. Who holds the San Francisco Giants season record for most innings pitched?

1. Vida Blue
2. Mike Krukow
3. Juan Marichal
4. Gaylord Perry
5. Rick Reuschel
6. Jack Sanford

719. Who holds the Minnesota Twins season record for most extra-base hits?

1. Harmon Killebrew
2. Chuck Knoblauch
3. Tony Oliva
4. Kirby Puckett

720. Who pitched the first perfect game in American League history?

1. Lefty Grove
2. Waite Hoyt
3. Walter Johnson
4. Addie Joss
5. Babe Ruth
6. Cy Young

721. Who holds the Baltimore Orioles career record for home runs?

1. Eddie Murray
2. Cal Ripken, Jr.
3. Brooks Robinson
4. Frank Robinson

722. Who was the first major leaguer to hit 2 home runs in one nine-inning game?

1. Cap Anson
2. Dennis Brouthers
3. Roger Connor
4. Hugh Duffy
5. George Hall
6. Honus Wagner

723. Who holds the major league record for most seasons leading his league in fewest strikeouts (150 or more games)?

1. Luke Appling
2. Nellie Fox
3. Joe Sewell
4. Lloyd Waner

724. Who holds the major league season record for most intentional bases on balls received?

1. Willie McCovey
2. Rogers Hornsby
3. Ralph Kiner
4. John Olerud
5. Babe Ruth
6. Ted Williams

725. Who holds the major league record for most seasons with 400 or more putouts by an outfielder?

1. Richie Ashburn
2. Garry Maddox
3. Willie Mays
4. Tris Speaker

726. Who holds the American League career record for most home runs by a third base-man?

1. Buddy Bell
2. George Brett
3. Graig Nettles
4. Dean Palmer
5. Brooks Robinson
6. Al Rosen

727. At the end of the 1998 season who was the active major league leader in steals of home?

1. Barry Bonds
2. Rickey Henderson
3. Kenny Lofton
4. Paul Molitor
5. Otis Nixon
6. Tim Raines

728. Who was the only man to hit for the cycle in the one-year existence of the Players League?

1. Roger Connor
2. Ed Delahanty
3. Buck Ewing
4. George Gore
5. Hank O'Day
6. Bill Shindle

729. Who holds the major league record for most consecutive years hitting 30 or more home runs?

1. Hank Aaron
2. Jimmie Foxx
3. Ralph Kiner
4. Eddie Mathews
5. Babe Ruth
6. Mike Schmidt

★ ◆ ★ ◆ ★

730. Which team holds the major league season record for most 1–0 games won?

1. Chicago White Sox
2. Los Angeles Dodgers
3. New York Giants
4. Pittsburgh Pirates
5. St. Louis Cardinals
6. Washington Senators

731. How many home runs did Babe Ruth hit with the Yankees?

1. 659
2. 672
3. 679
4. 686
5. 697
6. 708

732. Who holds the National League career record for most home runs by a switch-hitter?

1. Bobby Bonilla
2. Ken Caminiti
3. Howard Johnson
4. Pete Rose
5. Ted Simmons
6. Reggie Smith

733. Who was the last major leaguer to hit 4 triples in a nine-inning game?

1. Ty Cobb
2. Sam Crawford
3. Lance Johnson
4. Bill Joyce
5. Tris Speaker
6. Willie Wilson

734. Who holds the Chicago White Sox season record for most singles hit?

1. Luis Aparicio
2. Luke Appling
3. Eddie Collins
4. Joc Jackson
5. Lance Johnson
6. Minnie Minoso

735. Who was the first player to have 250 hits in a major league season?

1. Ty Cobb
2. Sam Crawford
3. Rogers Hornsby
4. George Sisler

736. Who holds the major league season record for most triples (36)?

1. Ty Cobb
2. Sam Crawford
3. Sam Rice
4. Wildfire Schulte
5. Honus Wagner
6. Owen Wilson

737. Who was the first batter to hit 10 home runs in a major league season?

1. Dan Brouthers
2. Jim O'Rourke
3. Harry Stovey
4. Ned Williamson

738. Who holds the Organized Baseball season record for most home runs (72)?

1. Buzz Arlett
2. Joe Baumann
3. Joe Hauser
4. Pete Incaviglia
5. Tony Lazzeri
6. Babe Ruth

739. Who holds the American League season record for most runs scored (177)?

1. Ty Cobb
2. Rickey Henderson
3. Babe Ruth
4. Ted Williams

740. Who was the first pitcher to win 10 or more games in relief in a major league season?

1. Elroy Face
2. Clark Griffith
3. Byron Houch
4. Wilcy Moore
5. Johnny Murphy
6. Elam Vangilder

741. Who was the first first baseman involved in more than 100 double plays as a fielder in a major league season?

1. Cap Anson
2. Charlie Comiskey
3. Mike Lehane
4. Stuffy McInnis

742. Who is the only man in Organized Baseball history to hit 60 or more home runs in a season twice?

1. Joe Baumann
2. Jose Canseco
3. Jimmie Foxx
4. Joe Hauser
5. Brad Komminsk
6. Dick Stuart

743. Who was the first shortstop with more than 600 assists in a major league season?

1. Dave Bancroft
2. Leo Cardenas
3. Rabbit Maranville
4. Cal Ripken, Jr.
5. Ozzie Smith
6. Glenn Wright

744. Who had the longest consecutive game hitting streak in Organized Baseball history (66 games)?

1. Joe DiMaggio
2. Tommy Holmes
3. Roman Mejias
4. Otto Pahlman
5. Joe Sewell
6. Joe Wilhoit

745. Who holds the record for most games played in the minor leagues without playing in the major leagues?

1. Larry Barton
2. Dick Gyselman
3. Spencer Harris
4. Arnold Statz
5. Bill Thomas
6. George Whiteman

746. Who was the first man in Organized Baseball history to hit 60 home runs in a season?

1. Frank Baker
2. Jake Bentley
3. Rogers Hornsby
4. Tony Lazzeri
5. Babe Ruth
6. George Sisler

747. Who was the first second baseman involved in more than 100 double plays as a fielder in a major league season?

1. Glenn Beckert
2. Bucky Harris
3. Bill Mazeroski
4. Bid McPhee
5. Jackie Robinson
6. Charlie Sweasy

748. Who was the first major league batter to strike out 100 times in his rookie season?

1. Bruce Campbell
2. Vince DiMaggio
3. George Grantham
4. Reggie Jackson
5. Tony Lazzeri
6. Jake Wood

749. Who was the first man to manage more than 2,000 major league games?

1. Cap Anson
2. John Clapp
3. Ned Hanlon
4. Connie Mack
5. Jim Mutrie
6. Harry Wright

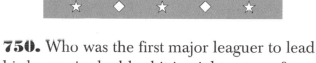

750. Who was the first major leaguer to lead his league in doubles hit in eight seasons?

1. Cap Anson
2. Ed Delahanty
3. Napoleon Lajoie
4. Bob Meusel
5. Socks Seybold
6. Tris Speaker
7. Honus Wagner

751. Who was the first major leaguer to lead his league in home runs hit in five seasons?

1. Frank Baker
2. Dan Brouthers
3. Ty Cobb
4. Gavvy Cravath
5. Babe Ruth
6. Harry Stovey

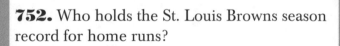

752. Who holds the St. Louis Browns season record for home runs?

1. Harlond Clift
2. Jeff Heath
3. Walt Judnich
4. Chet Laabs
5. George Sisler
6. Ken Williams

753. Who holds the original Washington Senators career record for home runs?

1. Goose Goslin
2. Harmon Killebrew
3. Roy Sievers
4. Mickey Vernon

754. Who holds the Atlanta Braves career record for home runs?

1. Hank Aaron
2. Darrell Evans
3. Ron Gant
4. Bob Horner
5. David Justice
6. Fred McGriff
7. Dale Murphy

755. Who holds the Minnesota Twins season record for home runs?

1. Tom Brunansky
2. Chili Davis
3. Kent Hrbek
4. Harmon Killebrew

756. Who holds the Milwaukee Brewers season record for home runs?

1. Rob Deer
2. Cecil Cooper
3. Ben Oglivie
4. Gorman Thomas
5. Greg Vaughn
6. Robin Yount

757. Who holds the Toronto Blue Jays career record for home runs?

1. George Bell
2. Joe Carter
3. Fred McGriff
4. Lloyd Moseby

758. Who holds the Toronto Blue Jays season record for home runs?

1. Jessie Barfield
2. George Bell
3. Joe Carter
4. Carlos Delgado
5. Cecil Fielder
6. Fred McGriff

759. Who holds the Boston Braves career record for home runs?

1. Hank Aaron
2. Wally Berger
3. Sid Gordon
4. Eddie Mathews

760. Who holds the Brooklyn Dodgers season record for home runs?

1. Roy Campanella
2. Carl Furillo
3. Babe Herman
4. Gil Hodges
5. Jackie Robinson
6. Duke Snider
7. Zack Wheat

761. Who holds the Cincinnati Reds season record for home runs?

1. Johnny Bench
2. George Foster
3. Ted Kluszewski
4. Ernie Lombardi
5. Lee May
6. Frank Robinson

762. Who holds the Houston Astros season record for home runs?

1. Moises Alou
2. Jeff Bagwell
3. Lee May
4. Joe Morgan
5. Rusty Staub
6. Jim Wynn

763. Who holds the Los Angeles Dodgers season record for home runs?

1. Ron Cey
2. Pedro Guerrero
3. Frank Howard
4. Mike Piazza
5. Reggie Smith
6. Darryl Strawberry

★　◆　★　◆　★

764. Who holds the Milwaukee Braves career record for home runs?

1. Hank Aaron
2. Joe Adcock
3. Del Crandall
4. Mack Jones
5. Eddie Mathews
6. Joe Torre

765. Who holds the Cleveland Indians season record for home runs?

1. Earl Averill, Sr.
2. Albert Belle
3. Rocky Colavito
4. Al Rosen
5. Jim Thome
6. Hal Trosky

766. Who holds the Chicago White Sox season record for home runs?

1. Dick Allen
2. Harold Baines
3. Albert Belle
4. Zeke Bonora
5. Frank Thomas
6. Robin Ventura

767. Who holds the Baltimore Orioles season record for home runs?

1. Brady Anderson
2. Eddie Murray
3. Rafael Palmeiro
4. Boog Powell
5. Cal Ripken, Jr.
6. Frank Robinson

768. Who holds the Angels season record for home runs?

1. Don Baylor
2. Chili Davis
3. Doug DeCinces
4. Brian Downing
5. Reggie Jackson
6. Tim Salmon

769. Who holds the Angels career record for home runs?

1. Don Baylor
2. Doug DeCinces
3. Brian Downing
4. Reggie Jackson
5. Fred Lynn
6. Tim Salmon

770. Who was the first player selected by the Kansas City Royals in the 1968 expansion draft?

1. Dick Drago
2. Joe Foy
3. Joe Keough
4. Roger Nelson
5. Jim Rooker
6. Jon Warden

771. Who holds the major league career record for most wins as a relief pitcher?

1. Dennis Eckersley
2. Roy Face
3. Kent Tekulve
4. Hoyt Wilhelm

772. Who holds the St. Louis Cardinals season record for most complete games pitched?

1. Grover Cleveland Alexander
2. Steve Carlton
3. Dizzy Dean
4. Bob Gibson
5. Joe Magrane
6. Jack W. Taylor
7. John Tudor

773. Who holds the major league career record for unassisted double plays as an out-fielder?

1. Dom DiMaggio
2. Hugh Duffy
3. Willie Mays
4. Tris Speaker

774. Who is the only major league pitcher to lead his league in wins eight times?

1. Lefty Grove
2. Walter Johnson
3. Jim Palmer
4. Amos Rusie
5. Warren Spahn
6. Cy Young

775. Which pitcher holds the New York Giants career record for bases on balls issued?

1. Carl Hubbell
2. Larry Jansen
3. Rube Marquard
4. Hal Schumacher

776. Who holds the major league record for shortstops for most assists in a game?

1. Rick Burleson
2. Bud Harrelson
3. Tony Kubek
4. Barry Larkin
5. Cal Ripken, Jr.
6. Ozzie Smith

777. Who holds the Chicago Cubs career record for most bases on balls received?

1. Ernie Banks
2. Stan Hack
3. Ron Santo
4. Billy Williams

778. Who is the only major league pitcher to lead his league in innings pitched seven times?

1. Grover Alexander
2. Pud Galvin
3. Walter Johnson
4. Warren Spahn
5. Don Sutton
6. Early Wynn

779. Who is the only major leaguer to twice steal two bases in an inning as a pinch-runner?

1. Pat Collins
2. Dave Concepcion
3. Allan Lewis
4. Bill O'Hara
5. Jake Pitler
6. Herb Washington

780. Who holds the major league season record for most bases on balls received as a pinch hitter?

1. Gates Brown
2. Smoky Burgess
3. Brian Harper
4. John Lowenstein
5. Dave Philley
6. Elmer Valo

781. Who holds the American League record for most stolen bases allowed by a catcher in one game?

1. Bill Carrigan
2. Jim Hegan
3. J.C. Martin
4. Steve O'Neill
5. Branch Rickey
6. Boss Schmidt

782. What's the longest 1–0 game in major league history?

1. 18 innings
2. 19 innings
3. 20 innings
4. 22 innings
5. 23 innings
6. 24 innings

783. Who holds the American League season record for runs scored?

1. Ty Cobb
2. Lou Gehrig
3. Rickey Henderson
4. Babe Ruth
5. Al Simmons
6. Willie Wilson

784. Who holds the major league record for most consecutive hits by a pinch-hitter?

1. Gates Brown
2. Sam Leslie
3. Manny Mota
4. Dave Philley
5. Del Unser
6. John Vander Wal

785. Who holds the American League season record for switch-hitters for most times hit by pitches?

1. Don Buford
2. Howard Johnson
3. Gene Larkin
4. Johnny Lucadello
5. Eddie Murray

★　◆　★　◆　★

786. Who holds the record for a major league catcher for the longest game with no passed balls?

1. Bob Boone
2. Carlton Fisk
3. Charles Johnson
4. Hal King
5. Al Lopez
6. Wally Schang

787. Who is the only major league pitcher with more than 3000 career strikeouts and fewer than 1000 bases on balls?

1. Bert Blyleven
2. Steve Carlton
3. Bob Gibson
4. Ferguson Jenkins
5. Don Sutton
6. Cy Young

★ ◆ ★ ◆ ★

788. Which team holds the record for most players used in a Division Series?

1. Atlanta Braves
2. Cleveland Indians
3. Florida Marlins
4. New York Yankees
5. Texas Ranger

789. Which team holds the record for most pinch hitters used in a Division Series?

1. Atlanta Braves
2. Boston Red Sox
3. Colorado Rockies
4. Florida Marlins

790. Which team holds the record for most Division Series played in?

1. Atlanta Braves
2. Cleveland Indians
3. Los Angeles Dodgers
4. New York Yankees
5. San Diego Padres
6. Seattle Mariners

791. Who holds the record for most runs scored in a Division Series?

   1. Dante Bichette
   2. Ken Griffey, Jr.
   3. Cal Ripken, Jr.
   4. Bernie Williams

792. Who holds the record for most hits in a Division Series game?

   1. Tony Armas
   2. Marquis Grissom
   3. Chipper Jones
   4. Edgar Martinez
   5. Don Mattingly
   6. Mark McLemore
   7. Bernie Williams

793. Who was the first batter to hit a grand slam in Division Series play?

1. Bobby Bonilla
2. Mark Lewis
3. Paul O'Neill
4. Devon White

794. Who was the first batter to hit a home run to lead off a Division Series game?

1. Brady Anderson
2. Marquis Grissom
3. Rickey Henderson
4. Derek Jeter
5. Chuck Knoblauch
6. Kenny Lofton
7. Jerry White

795. Who holds the record for most RBI in a Division Series?

1. Juan Gonzalez
2. Ken Griffey, Jr.
3. Edgar Martinez
4. Tino Martinez
5. Fred McGriff
6. Cal Ripken, Jr.

796. Which team holds the record for most home runs hit in a four-game Division Series?

1. Atlanta Braves
2. Baltimore Orioles
3. Cleveland Indians
4. Colorado Rockies
5. New York Yankees
6. Seattle Mariners

797. What is the record for most home runs hit by both teams in a Division Series?

  1. 13
  2. 15
  3. 16
  4. 17
  5. 18
  6. 22

798. Who holds the League Championship Series career record for most times hit by pitches?

  1. Don Baylor
  2. Rod Carew
  3. Lenny Dykstra
  4. Richie Hebner
  5. Walt Weiss

799. Who holds the record for most RBI in a League Championship Series?

1. Don Baylor
2. Juan Gonzalez
3. Reggie Jackson
4. Matt Williams

800. Who holds the National League League Championship Series career record for most stolen bases?

1. Barry Bonds
2. Brett Butler
3. Ron Gant
4. Davey Lopes
5. Willie McGee
6. Otis Nixon

801. Who is the only pitcher to hit a grand slam in a League Championship Series game?

1. Tony Cloninger
2. Mike Cuellar
3. Dave McNally
4. Tom Seaver

802. Who is the youngest player to pitch in a League Championship Series?

1. Bert Blyleven
2. Pat Dobson
3. Dwight Gooden
4. Don Gullett
5. Nolan Ryan
6. Todd Worrell

803. Who holds the record for the most positions played in one League Championship Series?

1. Pedro Guerrero
2. Lloyd McClendon
3. Pete Rose
4. Cesar Tovar

804. Who holds the record for the most times on the League Championship Series losing team?

1. Harold Baines
2. Bobby Bonds
3. Bobby Grich
4. Richie Hebner
5. Reggie Jackson
6. Greg Maddux

805. Who holds the National League record for most home runs in a League Championship Series game?

1. Jack Clark
2. Pedro Guerrero
3. Bob Robertson
4. Mike Schmidt

★ ◆ ★ ◆ ★

806. Who holds the record for most triples in a League Championship Series game?

1. Roberto Alomar
2. Ty Cline
3. Mariano Duncan
4. Rudy Law
5. Mark Lemke
6. Willie McGee
7. Willie Wilson

807. Who is the only pitcher to hit a bases-loaded triple in a League Championship Series game?

1. Ken Brett
2. Tom Glavine
3. Greg Maddux
4. Dave McNally
5. Jim Palmer
6. Fernando Valenzuela

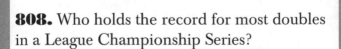

808. Who holds the record for most doubles in a League Championship Series?

1. Rod Carew
2. Ron Cey
3. Javier Lopez
4. Joe Morgan
5. Pete Rose
6. Bob Watson

809. Who holds the American League career record for most innings pitched in League Championship Series?

1. Roger Clemens
2. Ken Holtzman
3. Catfish Hunter
4. Dave McNally
5. Jim Palmer
6. Dave Stewart

810. Who holds the record for most singles in a League Championship Series?

1. Roberto Alomar
2. Paul Blair
3. Gary Matthews
4. Tim Raines
5. Joe Rudi
6. Jerome Walton

811. Who holds the League Championship Series career record for most games lost by a pitcher?

1. Doyle Alexander
2. Doug Drabek
3. Darold Knowles
4. Greg Maddux
5. Jerry Reuss
6. Don Sutton

812. Who holds the record for most hits in a League Championship Series game?

1. Paul Blair
2. Will Clark
3. Mark Grace
4. Gary Matthews
5. Paul Molitor
6. Bernie Williams

813. Who holds the World Series career record for most losses by a pitcher?

1. Whitey Ford
2. Walter Johnson
3. Red Ruffing
4. John Smoltz

814. Who holds the World Series career record for most games without a home run?

1. Frankie Frisch
2. Dal Maxvill
3. Phil Rizzuto
4. Bobby Richardson
5. Wally Schang
6. Enos Slaughter
7. Bucky Dent

815. Which pitcher holds the World Series record for most hit batters in one game?

1. Bob Gibson
2. Bruce Kison
3. Vic Raschi
4. Mitch Williams

816. Who holds the World Series career record for most sacrifices (bunts and flies)?

1. Mark Belanger
2. Eddie Collins
3. Dave Duncan
4. Tommy Herr
5. Pee Wee Reese
6. Steve Yeager

817. Who holds the Cincinnati Reds season record for most stolen bases?

1. Bob Bescher
2. Arlie Latham
3. Bid McPhee
4. Joe Morgan

818. Who holds the Milwaukee Braves season record for games won by a pitcher?

1. Vern Bickford
2. Bob Buhl
3. Lew Burdette
4. Tony Cloninger
5. Johnny Sain
6. Warren Spahn

819. Who holds the World Series career record for most innings pitched?

1. Whitey Ford
2. Catfish Hunter
3. Christy Mathewson
4. Red Ruffing

820. Who holds the New York Giants career record for most stolen bases?

1. George J. Burns
2. Art Devlin
3. Frankie Frisch
4. Willie Mays
5. Joe Moore
6. Fred Snodgrass
7. Monte Ward

821. Which pitcher holds the Philadelphia Athletics career record for most games won?

1. Jack Coombs
2. Lefty Grove
3. Eddie Plank
4. Rube Waddell

822. Who holds the New York Yankees season record for most sacrifice hits?

1. Ben Chapman
2. Joe Girardi
3. Lefty Gomez
4. Willie Keeler
5. Tony Kubek
6. Willie Randolph
7. Roy White

823. Who holds the Chicago Cubs career record for most stolen bases?

1. Cap Anson
2. Frank Chance
3. King Kelly
4. Bill Lange
5. Wildfire Schulte
6. Joe Tinker

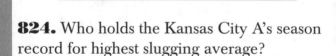

824. Who holds the Kansas City A's season record for highest slugging average?

1. Bob Cerv
2. Ed Charles
3. Rocky Colavito
4. Jim Gentile
5. Roger Maris
6. Vic Power

825. Who holds the Brooklyn Dodgers career record for most stolen bases?

1. Jake Daubert
2. Willie Keeler
3. Pee Wee Reese
4. Jackie Robinson
5. Jimmy Scheckard
6. Monte Ward

826. Who holds the Detroit Tigers record for consecutive wins by a pitcher?

1. Joe Coleman, Jr.
2. Hooks Dauss
3. Bill Donovan
4. Denny McLain
5. Hal Newhouser
6. Schoolboy Rowe

827. Who holds the Philadelphia Phillies season record for most stolen bases?

1. Richie Ashburn
2. Ed Delahanty
3. Lenny Dykstra
4. Billy Hamilton
5. Sherry Magee
6. Juan Samuel

828. Who holds the St. Louis Browns career record for most games pitched?

1. General Crowder
2. Dixie Davis
3. Bobo Newsom
4. Urban Shocker
5. Elam Vanglider
6. Rube Waddell

829. Who holds the Boston Braves career record for highest batting average?

1. Wally Berger
2. Hugh Duffy
3. Billy Hamilton
4. Tommy Holmes
5. Herman Long
6. Billy Southworth

830. Who holds the original Washington Senators season record for most runs scored?

1. George Case
2. Joe Cronin
3. Sam Rice
4. Roy Sievers
5. Mickey Vernon
6. Ed Yost

831. Which pitcher holds the World Series record for most hits allowed in one inning?

1. Walter Johnson
2. Don Newcombe
3. Allie Reynolds
4. Joe Wood

832. Who holds the World Series career record for most runs scored?

1. Yogi Berra
2. Mickey Mantle
3. Billy Martin
4. Joe Morgan
5. Stan Musial
6. Jackie Robinson

833. Which pitcher holds the record for most strikeouts in a World Series game?

1. Kevin Brown
2. Bob Gibson
3. Christy Mathewson
4. Jack Morris

834. Which manager holds the record for most World Series lost?

1. Walter Alston
2. Bobby Cox
3. Connie Mack
4. John McGraw
5. Casey Stengel
6. Earl Weaver

835. Who was the first National League player to score 4 runs in a World Series game?

1. Lou Brock
2. Pepper Martin
3. Enos Slaughter
4. Honus Wagner

836. Who holds the record for most putouts by a catcher in one World Series?

1. Yogi Berra
2. Jerry Grote
3. Elrod Hendricks
4. Terry Kennedy
5. Thurman Munson
6. John Roseboro

837. Who holds the record for most hits in World Series in consecutive years?

1. Paul Blair
2. Lou Brock
3. Billy Martin
4. Bobby Richardson

838. Who was the first player to steal home in a World Series game?

1. Ty Cobb
2. Kiki Cuyler
3. Bill Dahlen
4. Babe Dahlgren
5. George Davis
6. Jimmy Slagle

839. What is the only team playing in more than one World Series to win every Series it has played?

1. Boston Braves
2. Minnesota Twins
3. New York Mets
4. Toronto Blue Jays

★ ◆ ★ ◆ ★

840. Which team has lost the most World Series?

1. Brooklyn Dodgers
2. Boston Red Sox
3. Chicago Cubs
4. Detroit Tigers
5. New York Giants
6. New York Yankees
7. St. Louis Cardinals

841. Which pitcher holds the World Series career record for most consecutive games lost?

1. Joe Bush
2. Whitey Ford
3. Charlie Leibrandt
4. Don Newcombe
5. Eddie Plank
6. Joe Wood

★ ◆ ★ ◆ ★

842. Who holds the World Series career record for most games caught?

1. Johnny Bench
2. Yogi Berra
3. Mickey Cochrane
4. Bill Dickey
5. Johnny Kling
6. Wally Schang

843. Which pitcher has won the most shutouts in World Series play?

1. Rube Benton
2. Lefty Grove
3. Sandy Koufax
4. Christy Mathewson
5. Jim Palmer
6. Babe Ruth

844. Who is the last man with 3 pinch hits in one World Series?

1. John Blanchard
2. Ken Boswell
3. Mickey Hatcher
4. Gene Larkin
5. John Lowenstein
6. Lonnie Smith

845. Who is the oldest pitcher to start a World Series game?

1. Steve Carlton
2. Howard Ehmke
3. Orel Hershiser
4. Joe Niekro
5. Jack Quinn
6. Cy Young

846. Who holds the record for most RBI in one World Series?

1. Hank Bauer
2. Pat Duncan
3. Lou Gehrig
4. Reggie Jackson
5. Dale Murphy
6. Bobby Richardson

847. Who holds the World Series career record for most bases on balls received?

1. Eddie Collins
2. Joe DiMaggio
3. Lou Gehrig
4. Reggie Jackson
5. Mickey Mantle
6. Babe Ruth

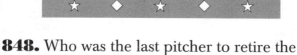

848. Who was the last pitcher to retire the side on three pitches in a World Series game?

1. Tiny Bonham
2. Whitey Ford
3. Christy Mathewson
4. Red Ruffing
5. Hippo Vaughn
6. Rube Walberg

849. What franchise has lost the most World Series?

1. Red Sox
2. Dodgers
3. Yankees
4. Cardinals

850. When was the last time there were three consecutive World Series with no shutouts?

1. 1919–21
2. 1927–30
3. 1936–38
4. 1942–45
5. 1958–60
6. 1976–78
7. 1980–82

851. Who is the only outfielder with 30 putouts in one World Series?

1. Joe DiMaggio
2. Kenny Lofton
3. Willie McGee
4. Edd Roush

852. Who is the last non-first baseman to turn an unassisted double play in a World Series game?

1. Greg Gagne
2. Joe Girardi
3. Mark Lemke
4. Pete Rose
5. Walt Weiss
6. Frank White

853. Who is the youngest man to manage a World Series-winning team?

1. Sparky Anderson
2. Lou Boudreau
3. Joe Cronin
4. Bucky Harris

854. What was the first team to win a World Series with 4–0 sweep?

1. Boston Red Sox
2. Boston Braves
3. Chicago Cubs
4. Cleveland Indians
5. New York Giants
6. New York Yankees
7. Pittsburgh Pirates

855. What was the first team to win World Series 4–0 in consecutive years?

1. Chicago Cubs
2. New York Giants
3. New York Yankees
4. Philadelphia Athletics

856. Which team has played the most tie games in World Series history?

1. Brooklyn Dodgers
2. Cicinnati Reds
3. Detroit Tigers
4. New York Giants
5. Philadelphia Athletics
6. St. Louis Cardinals
7. Washington Senators

857. Who holds the World Series record for most doubles hit in one game?

1. Pete Fox
2. Chick Hafey
3. Billy Hatcher
4. Frank Isbell

858. Who is the last player to hit two triples in one World Series game?

1. Tommy Davis
2. Greg Gagne
3. Dan Gladden
4. Rickey Henderson
5. Mark Lemke
6. Bobby Richardson
7. Andy Van Slyke

859. Who was the first man to manage three different teams in the World Series?

1. Sparky Anderson
2. Lou Boudreau
3. Bucky Harris
4. Bill McKechnie
5. Joe Torre
6. Dick Williams

860. What year was the first World Series night game?

1. 1938
2. 1949
3. 1957
4. 1969
5. 1971
6. 1973

861. What was the last team to play an error-less World Series?

1. Baltimore Orioles, 1966
2. Chicago Cubs, 1907
3. New York Giants, 1912
4. New York Yankees, 1927
5. New York Yankees, 1937
6. Philadelphia Phillies, 1950

862. What was the first team to play an errorless World Series?

1. Baltimore Orioles, 1966
2. Chicago Cubs, 1907
3. New York Giants, 1912
4. New York Yankees, 1927
5. New York Yankees, 1937
6. Philadelphia Phillies, 1950

863. Who holds the World Series career record for most runners caught stealing by a catcher?

1. Johnny Bench
2. Yogi Berra
3. Roy Campanella
4. Mickey Cochrane
5. Wally Schang

★　◆　★　◆　★

864. Who holds the World Series career record for most fielding chances accepted by a pitcher?

1. Whitey Ford
2. Bob Gibson
3. Lefty Gomez
4. Lefty Grove
5. Catfish Hunter
6. Christy Mathewson

865. Among American League teams, which franchise has the highest winning percentage in World Series games?

1. Athletics/A's
2. Blue Jays
3. Browns/Orioles
4. Senators/Twins
5. Yankees

866. Among National League teams, which franchise has the highest winning percentage in World Series games?

1. Cardinals
2. Cubs
3. Dodgers
4. Giants
5. Marlins
6. Mets

867. Who holds the career record for most extra bases on extra-base hits?

1. Hank Aaron
2. Ty Cobb
3. Willie Mays
4. Babe Ruth

868. Who holds the major league season record for most games started as a pitcher?

1. Jack Chesbro
2. Walter Johnson
3. Christy Mathewson
4. Kid Nichols
5. "Hoss" Radbourne
6. Will White
7. Cy Young

869. Who holds the major league season record for most consecutive errorless games played at third base?

1. Clete Boyer
2. Jim Davenport
3. Don Money
4. Brooks Robinson

870. What is the most runs scored by both teams in the first inning of a major league game?

1. 15
2. 16
3. 17
4. 18
5. 19
6. 20

871. Who was the Boston manager the last time the Red Sox won a World Series?

1. Ed Barrow
2. Bill Carrigan
3. Jimmy Collins
4. Patsy Donovan

872. Who holds the American League season record for most games by a pinch-hitter?

1. Benny Ayala
2. Gates Brown
3. Smoky Burgess
4. Dave Philley
5. Tim Raines
6. Elmer Valo

873. Who holds the major league record for most times grounding into a double play in two consecutive games?

1. Zeke Bonura
2. George Kurowski
3. Ernie Lombardi
4. Joe Torre

874. Which pitcher holds the National League season record for most hit batsmen?

1. Don Drysdale
2. Bob Gibson
3. Juan Marichal
4. Pedro Martinez
5. Joe McGinnity
6. J.R. Richard

875. Who is the only shortstop to play an 18-inning doubleheader with no chances offered?

1. Luis Aparicio
2. Greg Gagne
3. Toby Harrah
4. Roy Smalley

876. From 1903 through 1947, how many men managed the New York Giants?

1. 1
2. 2
3. 3
4. 4
5. 5
6. 6
7. 7

877. Who holds the record for most seasons leading his league in lowest earned-run average?

1. Grover Alexander
2. Bob Gibson
3. Lefty Grove
4. Walter Johnson
5. Sandy Koufax
6. Ed Walsh

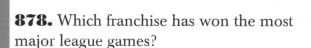

878. Which franchise has won the most major league games?

1. Braves
2. Cardinals
3. Cubs
4. Dodgers
5. Giants
6. Yankees

879. Who was the last major leaguer to lead the his league in slugging average four consecutive seasons?

1. Jimmie Foxx
2. Reggie Jackson
3. Mickey Mantle
4. Babe Ruth
5. Mike Schmidt
6. Ted Williams

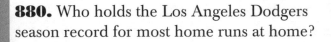

880. Who holds the Los Angeles Dodgers season record for most home runs at home?

1. Ron Cey
2. Pedro Guerrero
3. Mike Marshall
4. Mike Piazza
5. Reggie Smith
6. Darryl Strawberry

881. Who holds the season record for most games played by a lefthanded shortstop?

1. Jim Brody
2. Al Garvey
3. Billy Hulen
4. Dale Long
5. Howard Nolan
6. Chickenlegs Staley

882. Who was the first player to hit a pinch home run in his first major league at-bat?

1. Gates Brown
2. John Kennedy
3. Les Leyton
4. Eddie Morgan
5. Ace Parker
6. Chuck Tanner
7. Ted Tappe

883. What is the only franchise to hit five home runs in an inning twice?

1. Cubs
2. Dodgers
3. Giants
4. Mariners
5. Rockies
6. Yankees

884. Who was the last player to lead the National League in games played at shortstop six seasons?

1. Dick Bartell
2. Larry Bowa
3. Rabbit Maranville
4. Roy McMillan
5. Ozzie Smith
6. Arky Vaughan

885. Who holds the Boston Red Sox season record for most bases on balls received?

1. Jimmie Foxx
2. Jim Rice
3. Mo Vaughn
4. Ted Williams

886. Who holds the Boston Red Sox season record for most RBI?

1. Dwight Evans
2. Jimmie Foxx
3. Jim Rice
4. Vern Stephens
5. Mo Vaughn
6. Ted Williams
7. Carl Yastrezemski

887. Which pitcher holds the Baltimore Orioles season record for most shutouts?

1. Mike Cuellar
2. Dave McNally
3. Mike Mussina
4. Jim Palmer

888. Who holds the Philadelphia Athletics career record for most games played?

1. Mickey Cochrane
2. Harry Davis
3. Jimmie Dykes
4. Jimmie Foxx
5. Dick Siebert
6. Al Simmons

889. Who was the first player to hit five grand slams as a Met?

1. Tommie Agee
2. Howard Johnson
3. John Milner
4. Darryl Strawberry

890. Who holds the Cincinnati Reds season record for most total bases?

1. Johnny Bench
2. Eric Davis
3. George Foster
4. Dave Parker
5. Frank Robinson
6. Pete Rose

891. How many seasons have the Philadelphia Phillies finished with a winning in the 1990s?

1. 1
2. 2
3. 3
4. 4

892. Who holds the Milwaukee Brewers career record for most doubles?

1. Cecil Cooper
2. Jim Gantner
3. Paul Molitor
4. Ben Oglivie
5. Gorman Thomas
6. Robin Yount

893. How many times have the Detroit Tigers finished first?

   1. 7
   2. 9
   3. 11
   4. 13

894. How many winning seasons did the Cleveland Indians have from 1960 through 1990?

   1. 4
   2. 5
   3. 6
   4. 7
   5. 8
   6. 9
   7. 10

895. Which pitcher holds the Chicago Cubs career record (since 1900) for most complete games?

1. Grover Alexander
2. Mordecai Brown
3. Ferguson Jenkins
4. Ed Reulbach
5. Rick Reuschel
6. Rick Sutcliffe

896. Who holds the Atlanta Braves season record for most bases on balls received?

1. Hank Aaron
2. Darrell Evans
3. Bob Horner
4. Ryan Klesko
5. Dale Murphy
6. Jim Wynn

897. Who holds the New York Yankees record for most consecutive games driving in a run?

1. Yogi Berra
2. Lou Gehrig
3. Mickey Mantle
4. Don Mattingly
5. Babe Ruth
6. Dave Winfield

★ ◆ ★ ◆ ★

898. Who holds the Philadelphia Phillies career record for most stolen bases?

1. Richie Ashburn
2. Ed Delahanty
3. Billy Hamilton
4. Sherry Magee
5. Juan Samuel
6. Roy Thomas

899. Who holds the Brooklyn Dodgers season record for most at-bats?

1. Hub Collins
2. Carl Furillo
3. Babe Herman
4. Gil Hodges
5. Jackie Robinson
6. Duke Snider

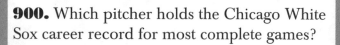

900. Which pitcher holds the Chicago White Sox career record for most complete games?

1. Wilson Alvarez
2. Ed Cicotte
3. Red Faber
4. Jack Harshman
5. Dickie Kerr
6. Ted Lyons

901. Which pitcher holds the Oakland A's record for most strikeouts in a game?

1. Vida Blue
2. Catfish Hunter
3. Ken Holtzman
4. Matt Keough
7. Dave Stewart
8. Bob Welch

902. What was the first year the Montreal Expos finished the season with a winning record?

1. 1971
2. 1973
3. 1975
4. 1977
5. 1979
6. 1980

903. Who is the only man to pitch in 27 major league seasons?

1. Dennis Eckersley
2. Tommy John
3. Dennis Martinez
4. Nolan Ryan

904. How many seasons did Babe Ruth lead American League batters in strikeouts?

1. 5
2. 6
3. 7
4. 8
5. 9
6. 10
7. 11

905. Which pitcher holds the National League career record for most innings pitched?

1. Mordecai Brown
2. Steve Carlton
3. Nolan Ryan
4. Warren Spahn

★ ◆ ★ ◆ ★

906. Who is the last major leaguer to lead his league in RBI three consecutive seasons?

1. Albert Belle
2. Barry Bonds
3. Cecil Fielder
4. George Foster
5. Ken Griffey, Jr.
6. Jim Rice
7. Frank Thomas

907. Who was the first National Leaguer to turn an unassisted triple play?

1. Jimmy Cooney
2. Mickey Morandini
3. Ernie Padgett
4. Glenn Wright

908. What is the only major league franchise to hit four home runs in an inning six times in its history?

1. Braves
2. Giants
3. Indians
4. Red Sox
5. Twins
6. Yankees

909. Who was the the last pitcher to lead or tie for the lead in strikeouts four consecutive seasons in the National League?

1. Dizzy Dean
2. Robin Roberts
3. Tom Seaver
4. Warren Spahn

910. Who was the first pitcher to lead the American League in strikeouts six consecutive seasons?

1. Bob Feller
2. Lefty Grove
3. Walter Johnson
4. Red Ruffing
5. Rube Waddell
6. Cy Young

911. Who was the first American League pitcher to throw more than 10 shutouts in a season?

1. Lefty Grove
2. Walter Johnson
3. Ed Walsh, Sr.
4. Cy Young

912. Who was the first player to lead the American League in stolen bases five consecutive seasons?

1. Harry Bay
2. George Case
3. Ben Chapman
4. Ty Cobb
5. Eddie Collins
6. Clyde Milan

913. Who was the first National Leaguer to hit more than 40 home runs in one season?

1. Gavvy Cravath
2. Rogers Hornsby
3. Chuck Klein
4. Mel Ott
5. Cy Williams
6. Hack Wilson

914. Who was the first player to lead the National League in batting average two consecutive seasons?

1. Cap Anson
2. Dan Brouthers
3. Hugh Duffy
4. George Gore
5. Willie Keeler
6. Jim O'Rourke

915. Who was the last major leaguer to lead his league in bases on balls received four consecutive seasons?

1. Barry Bonds
2. Babe Ruth
3. Mike Schmidt
4. Frank Thomas
5. Ted Williams

916. Before Babe Ruth broke it, who held the American League season record for home runs with 16?

1. Home Run Baker
2. Sam Crawford
3. Buck Freeman
4. Napoleon Lajoie
5. Socks Seybold
6. Tilly Walker

917. Who is the only major leaguer to lead his league in stolen bases nine consecutive seasons?

1. Luis Aparicio
2. Lou Brock
3. Ty Cobb
4. Billy Hamilton
5. Rickey Henderson

918. Who was the first player to lead the National League in doubles four consecutive seasons?

1. Cap Anson
2. Ross Barnes
3. Dan Brouthers
4. Ed Delahanty
5. Rogers Hornsby
6. Honus Wagner

919. Who is the only man to lead the American League in triples with as few as 8 in a season?

1. Hank Bauer
2. John Castino
3. Carlton Fisk
4. Gil McDougald
5. Del Unser

★ ◆ ★ ◆ ★

920. Who was the last man to lead the American League in home runs with less than 10 in a season?

1. Home Run Baker
2. Ty Cobb
3. Harry Davis
4. Wally Pipp
5. Braggo Roth
6. Babe Ruth

921. Who is the only player to win the MVP award in both the American and National Leagues?

1. Dick Allen
2. Roger Maris
3. Mark McGwire
4. Frank Robinson

★　◆　★　◆　★

922. Who is the only major leaguer to lead his league in total bases in eight seasons?

1. Hank Aaron
2. Reggie Jackson
3. Mickey Mantle
4. Willie Mays
5. Babe Ruth
6. Mike Schmidt

923. Who is the only major league first base-man to lead his league in fielding percentage five consecutive seasons?

1. Steve Garvey
2. Ted Kluszewski
3. John Olerud
4. Vic Power

924. Who holds the National League career record for most putouts by a third baseman?

1. Ron Cey
2. Eddie Mathews
3. Ron Santo
4. Mike Schmidt
5. Pie Traynor
6. Tim Wallach

925. Who replaced Lou Gehrig in the Yankees lineup the day his consecutive games played streak ended?

1. Babe Dahlgren
2. Joe Gordon
3. Tommy Henrich
4. Wally Pipp

926. Who holds the American League career record for most home runs by a second baseman?

1. Roberto Alomar
2. Bobby Doerr
3. Joe Gordon
4. Bobby Grich
5. Lou Whitaker
6. Frank White

927. Who is the only major leaguer to hit 20 or more triples in five seasons?

1. Ty Cobb
2. Sam Crawford
3. Kenny Lofton
4. Willie Wilson

928. What is the major league record for fewest hits allowed by a pitcher pitching all 18 innings of a doubleheader?

1. 2
2. 3
3. 4
4. 5
5. 6
6. 7
7. 8

929. Who was the last pitcher to win 20 games in his rookie major league season?

1. Vida Blue
2. Tom Browning
3. Dwight Gooden
4. Kerry Wood

930. What is the shortest time in which a nine-inning major league game has been completed?

1. 47 minutes
2. 49 minutes
3. 51 minutes
4. 53 minutes
5. 55 minutes
6. 58 minutes
7. 61 minutes

931. Who was the first National Leaguer to hit 30 or more home runs and steal 30 or more bases in one season?

1. Hank Aaron
2. Bobby Bonds
3. Willie Mays
4. Joe Medwick
5. Honus Wagner

932. How many players hit for the cycle twice in the history of the American Association (1882–91)?

1. 1
2. 2
3. 3
4. 4
5. 5
6. 6

933. Who was the first batter to homer in his first two major league at-bats?

1. Ron Blomberg
2. Bobby Bonds
3. Clint Hartung
4. Bob Nieman
5. Juan Samuel
6. Mike Schmidt

934. Who is the only National Leaguer to strike out six times in one game (extra innings)?

1. Richie Allen
2. Rob Deer
3. Don Hoak
4. Pete Incaviglia
5. Frank Tavares
6. Billy Sunday

935. Who holds the National League season record for most consecutive games without striking out?

1. Matty Alou
2. Richie Ashburn
3. Tony Gwynn
4. Stan Musial
5. Lloyd Waner

936. Who holds the American League career record for most strikeouts by a lefthanded pitcher?

1. Lefty Gomez
2. Lefty Grove
3. Randy Johnson
4. Walter Johnson
5. Mark Langston
6. Mickey Lolich

937. Which franchise holds the major league career record for most games lost?

1. Browns/Orioles
2. Cardinals
3. Cubs
4. Giants
5. Phillies

938. Which team holds the major league record for most consecutive games won, with no ties, in a season (21)?

1. Cincinnati Reds
2. Chicago Cubs
3. Cleveland Indians
4. Detroit Tigers
5. New York Giants
6. New York Yankees
7. Pittsburgh Pirates

939. Which pitcher holds the Kansas City Royals season record for longest winning streak?

1. Bud Black
2. Dick Drago
3. Rich Gale
4. Mark Gubicza
5. Bret Saberhagen
6. Paul Splittorff

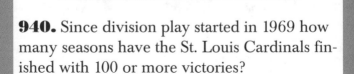

940. Since division play started in 1969 how many seasons have the St. Louis Cardinals finished with 100 or more victories?

1. 0
2. 1
3. 2
4. 3
5. 4

941. What year did the Minnesota Twins first finish with a record above .500?

1. 1962
2. 1963
3. 1964
4. 1968
5. 1976
6. 1987

942. Who holds the Chicago Cubs career record for highest batting average?

1. Cap Anson
2. Ernie Banks
3. Frank Chance
4. Max Flack
5. Mark Grace
6. Billy Herman

943. Who was the modern Milwaukee Brewers manager the year the club had its first winning season?

1. George Bamberger
2. Dave Bristol
3. Del Crandell
4. Phil Garner
5. Harvey Kuenn
6. Buck Rodgers

944. Who was the last man to play more than 162 games in a season for the Pittsburgh Pirates?

1. Barry Bonds
2. Bobby Bonilla
3. Phil Garner
4. Bill Mazeroski
5. Al Oliver
6. Johnny Rizzo

945. Which year did the New York Highlanders team first lose more than 100 games?

1. 1902
2. 1904
3. 1908
4. 1910
5. 1912
6. 1914

946. What was the first year the New York Mets finished the season with less than 100 losses?

1. 1964
2. 1965
3. 1966
4. 1967
5. 1968
6. 1969

947. How many games out of first place did the Seattle Pilots finish in the team's only major league season?

1. 18
2. 29
3. 33
4. 34
5. 37
6. 41

948. Who holds the Kansas City A's season record for most sacrifice hits?

1. Ed Charles
2. Rocky Colavito
3. Alvin Dark
4. Jerry Lumpe
5. Norm Siebern
6. Dick Williams

949. Who holds the New York Giants season record for most extra-base hits by a batter?

1. George Davis
2. Larry Doyle
3. Sid Gordon
4. Willie Mays
5. Mel Ott
6. Hack Wilson

950. Who was the manager the year the AL Detroit Tigers franchise had its first winning season?

1. Bill Armour
2. Ed Barrow
3. Frank Dwyer
4. Hughey Jennings
5. Bobby Lowe
6. George Stallings

951. Who holds the Montreal Expos season record for most hits by a batter?

1. Warren Cromartie
2. Andre Dawson
3. Al Oliver
4. Tim Raines
5. Rusty Staub
6. Tim Wallach

952. Which American League team was the first to hit three consecutive home runs in one inning?

1. Boston
2. Chicago
3. Cleveland
4. Detroit
5. New York
6. Philadelphia

953. How many losing seasons did the Braves have while based in Milwaukee?

1. 0
2. 1
3. 2
4. 3
5. 4
6. 5

954. Which AL team finished first in the American League's inaugural season?

1. Baltimore
2. Boston
3. Chicago
4. Cleveland
5. Detroit
6. Washington

955. What was the Dodgers' first season of 100 or more wins after moving to Los Angeles?

1. 1960
2. 1961
3. 1962
4. 1963
5. 1964
6. 1965

956. What year did the Baltimore Orioles franchise have its first winning record after moving from St. Louis?

1. 1955
2. 1956
3. 1957
4. 1958
5. 1959
6. 1960

957. Who was the first American League player to hit a home run in his first major league at-bat?

1. Mike Grady
2. Napoleon Lajoie
3. John McGraw
4. Ace Parker
5. Babe Ruth
6. Luke Stuart

958. Who holds the major league record for most years leading his league's first basemen in assists?

1. Jake Beckley
2. Don Mattingly
3. George Scott
4. George Sisler
5. Fred Tenney

959. Who holds the major league season record for fewest strikeouts by a switch-hitter playing a minimum of 150 games?

1. Frankie Frisch
2. Howard Johnson
3. Mickey Mantle
4. Eddie Murray
5. Pete Rose
6. Joe Sewell

★ ◆ ★ ◆ ★

960. Who was the last American League pitcher to win 17 games in relief in one season?

1. Bill Campbell
2. Ron Davis
3. Jerry Don Gleaton
4. John Hiller
5. Wilcy Moore
6. Hoyt Wilhelm

961. What is the record for most major leagues played in by a ballplayer?

1. 3
2. 4
3. 5
4. 6
5. 7
6. 8

962. Who was the first major league batter to receive 7 consecutive bases on balls?

1. Jose Canseco
2. Jack Clark
3. Rogers Hornsby
4. Mel Ott
5. Billy Rogell
6. Eddie Stanky

963. Who is the only shortstop with nine putouts but no assists in a major league game?

1. Monte Cross
2. Bill Dahlen
3. Buck Herzog
4. Shorty Fuller
5. Bud Harrelson
6. Ozzie Smith

964. Who was the first major leaguer to hit four home runs in a doubleheader (with home runs in each game)?

1. Earl Averill
2. Jimmy Foxx
3. Charlie Gehringer
4. Stan Musial
5. Babe Ruth
6. Jim Tabor

965. Who holds the major league season record for most chances accepted by a pitcher with a 1.000 fielding average?

1. Lefty Grove
2. Walter Johnson
3. Randy Jones
4. Greg Maddux
5. Tom Seaver

966. Who was the first American League player to lead the league in batting average in a year he played on two different teams?

1. Dale Alexander
2. Ed Delahanty
3. Lew Fonseca
4. Goose Goslin
5. Buddy Myer
6. George Stirnweiss

967. Who was the first National Leaguer to be caught stealing twice in one inning?

1. Vince Coleman
2. Richie Hebner
3. Jim Morrison
4. Donell Nixon
5. Paul Noce
6. Maury Wills

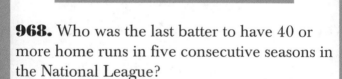

968. Who was the last batter to have 40 or more home runs in five consecutive seasons in the National League?

1. Hank Aaron
2. Rogers Hornsby
3. Ralph Kiner
4. Dale Murphy
5. Mike Schmidt
6. Duke Snider

969. Who was the first major leaguer to play all nine positions in one season?

1. Sport McAllister
2. Bert Campaneris
3. Sam Mertes
4. Gene Paulette
5. Cesar Tovar
6. Jimmy M.T. Walsh

★ ◆ ★ ◆ ★

970. Who was the last player to play for 10 major league teams?

1. Pete Appleton
2. Ken Brett
3. Sam P. Jones
4. Bob L. Miller
5. Ken Sanders
6. Harry Simpson

971. Who was the first batter to reach base via fielding error twice in one inning?

1. Johnny Bassler
2. Ty Cobb
3. Napoleon Lajoie
4. Sam Rice
5. Emory Rigney
6. Fred Spurgeon

★ ◆ ★ ◆ ★

972. Who holds the American League season record for most losses by a rookie pitcher?

1. Terry Felton
2. Bob Groom
3. Alex Kellner
4. Jack Nabors
5. Pedro Ramos
6. Dizzy Trout

973. Who holds the major league career record for most unassisted double plays by an outfielder?

1. Paul Blair
2. Max Carey
3. Ty Cobb
4. Happy Felsch
5. Willie Mays
6. Tris Speaker

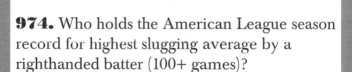

974. Who holds the American League season record for highest slugging average by a righthanded batter (100+ games)?

1. Jimmie Foxx
2. Lou Gehrig
3. Ken Griffey, Jr
4. Mickey Mantle
5. Babe Ruth

975. Who was the first Philadelphia Phillie to win a Gold Glove award?

1. Richie Ashburn
2. Von Hayes
3. Robin Roberts
4. Mike Schmidt
5. Bobby Shantz
6. Bobby Wine

976. Who was the Seattle Mariners' first All-Star?

1. Ken Griffey, Jr.
2. Ruppert Jones
3. Craig Reynolds
4. Enrique Romo
5. Lee Stanton
6. Richie Zisk

977. Who was the first Pittsburgh Pirate to win the Cy Young award?

1. Doug Drabek
2. Elroy Face
3. Bob Friend
4. Vernon Law
5. Vinegar Bend Mizell
6. Bob Veale

978. Who is the only Dodger pitcher to win two complete games in one day?

1. Oscar Jones
2. Sandy Koufax
3. Rube Marquard
4. Patrick Ragan
5. Bill Scanlan
6. Dazzy Vance

979. Who was the first Cleveland Indian to win the MVP award?

   1. Albert Belle
   2. Lou Boudreau
   3. Rocky Colavito
   4. George Burns
   5. Bob Johnson
   6. Al Rosen

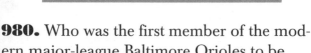

980. Who was the first member of the modern major-league Baltimore Orioles to be elected to the Hall of Fame?

   1. Luis Aparicio
   2. George Kell
   3. Ted Kluszewski
   4. Jim Palmer
   5. Robin Roberts
   6. Frank Robinson

981. Who was the first NY Yankee to lead the AL in home runs?

1. Frank Baker
2. Hal Chase
3. Lou Gehrig
4. Tony Lazzeri
5. Wally Pipp
6. Babe Ruth

982. Who pitched the first no-hitter for the Giants?

1. Leon Ames
2. Ed Crane
3. Cecil Ferguson
4. Christy Mathewson
5. Joe McGinnity
6. Amos Rusie

983. Who was the first Milwaukee Brewer to have 200 hits in a season?

1. Cecil Cooper
2. Tommy Harper
3. Paul Molitor
4. Ben Ogilvie
5. George Scott
6. Robin Yount

984. Who was the first player selected by the San Diego Padres in the 1968 expansion draft?

1. Jose Arcia
2. Ollie Brown
3. Nate Colbert
4. Dave Giusti
5. Clay Kirby
6. Jerry Morales

985. Who was the first Toronto Blue Jay to hit two home runs in a game?

1. Alan Ashby
2. Doug Ault
3. Bob Bailor
4. Ron Fairly
5. Roy Howell
6. Otto Velez

986. When the Minnesota Twins turned their first triple play, who was the batter?

1. Mike Epstein
2. Willie Horton
3. Frank Malzone
4. Roger Maris
5. Rich Reichardt
6. Danny Wilson

987. Who was the first Detroit Tiger to hit for the cycle?

1. Ty Cobb
2. Sam Crawford
3. Bob Fothergill
4. Charlie Gehringer
5. Bobby Veach
6. Gee Walker

Answers

The answers are arranged by tens, starting
with numbers ending in one and ending with
numbers ending in zero.

1. 1	161. 3	321. 6	481. 4	641. 4
11. 5	171. 1	331. 4	491. 3	651. 5
21. 3	181. 1	341. 2	501. 1	661. 2
31. 6	191. 6	351. 5	511. 1	671. 2
41. 4	201. 4	361. 2	521. 2	681. 6
51. 6	211. 4	371. 2	531. 5	691. 1
61. 4	221. 2	381. 3	541. 3	701. 1
71. 5	231. 4	391. 3	551. 1	711. 1
81. 4	241. 1	401. 3	561. 1	721. 2
91. 3	251. 6	411. 2	571. 3	731. 1
101. 1	261. 3	421. 2	581. 6	741. 2
111. 4	271. 1	431. 6	591. 1	751. 6
121. 2	281. 3	441. 4	601. 3	761. 2
131. 1	291. 4	451. 2	611. 4	771. 4
141. 5	301. 5	461. 6	621. 3	781. 5
151. 3	311. 3	471. 3	631. 2	791. 2

801. 2	42. 3	272. 5	502. 3	732. 1
811. 5	52. 3	282. 2	512. 4	742. 4
821. 3	62. 4	292. 1	522. 5	752. 6
831. 4	72. 6	302. 4	532. 6	762. 2
841. 1	82. 2	312. 5	542. 3	772. 6
851. 4	92. 6	322. 5	552. 4	782. 6
861. 1	102. 5	332. 1	562. 6	792. 2
871. 1	112. 3	342. 2	572. 6	802. 1
881. 3	122. 3	352. 5	582. 3	812. 1
891. 1	132. 2	362. 3	592. 1	822. 4
901. 1	142. 2	372. 1	602. 2	832. 2
911. 3	152. 3	382. 6	612. 4	842. 2
921. 4	162. 6	392. 3	622. 4	852. 3
931. 3	172. 6	402. 2	632. 3	862. 5
941. 1	182. 6	412. 6	642. 1	872. 6
951. 3	192. 4	422. 4	652. 1	882. 4
961. 4	202. 6	432. 6	662. 5	892. 6
971. 5	212. 4	442. 2	672. 6	902. 5
981. 5	222. 2	452. 4	682. 1	912. 2
2. 5	232. 6	462. 2	692. 4	922. 1
12. 2	242. 4	472. 5	702. 3	932. 4
22. 3	252. 1	482. 3	712. 1	942. 1
32. 3	262. 2	492. 5	722. 5	952. 3

962. 5	203. 1	433. 4	663. 5	893. 3
972. 2	213. 6	443. 3	673. 2	903. 4
982. 2	223. 2	453. 1	683. 1	913. 2
3. 3	233. 6	463. 1	693. 3	923. 2
13. 4	243. 2	473. 6	703. 4	933. 4
23. 4	253. 1	483. 4	713. 5	943. 1
33. 3	263. 2	493. 1	723. 2	953. 1
43. 4	273. 4	503. 2	733. 4	963. 3
53. 4	283. 5	513. 4	743. 6	973. 6
63. 3	293. 3	523. 2	753. 3	983. 1
73. 1	303. 4	533. 3	763. 4	4. 2
83. 5	313. 4	543. 5	773. 4	14. 2
93. 4	323. 6	553. 4	783. 4	24. 1
103. 1	333. 1	563. 3	793. 2	34. 2
113. 4	343. 2	573. 1	803. 4	44. 3
123. 5	353. 3	583. 4	813. 1	54. 3
133. 3	363. 2	593. 1	823. 2	64. 1
143. 1	373. 1	603. 2	833. 2	74. 3
153. 2	383. 1	613. 2	843. 4	84. 6
163. 4	393. 6	623. 2	853. 4	94. 2
173. 3	403. 4	633. 2	863. 5	104. 1
183. 2	413. 6	643. 2	873. 1	114. 4
193. 4	423. 5	653. 2	883. 3	124. 6

134. 3	364. 4	594. 2	824. 1	65. 1
144. 2	374. 1	604. 4	834. 4	75. 3
154. 1	384. 5	614. 1	844. 2	85. 2
164. 3	394. 5	624. 1	854. 3	95. 2
174. 2	404. 4	634. 1	864. 6	105. 5
184. 4	414. 6	644. 3	874. 5	115. 1
194. 3	424. 4	654. 5	884. 4	125. 4
204. 2	434. 4	664. 5	894. 6	135. 5
214. 1	444. 5	674. 4	904. 1	145. 4
224. 2	454. 3	684. 4	914. 2	155. 4
234. 1	464. 4	694. 2	924. 5	165. 3
244. 1	474. 6	704. 4	934. 3	175. 3
254. 4	484. 6	714. 3	944. 2	185. 1
264. 4	494. 1	724. 1	954. 3	195. 4
274. 4	504. 6	734. 3	964. 1	205. 2
284. 3	514. 5	744. 6	974. 1	215. 4
294. 4	524. 5	754. 7	984. 2	225. 3
304. 5	534. 5	764. 5	5. 3	235. 2
314. 4	544. 1	774. 5	15. 4	245. 3
324. 2	554. 5	784. 4	25. 3	255. 2
334. 6	564. 3	794. 2	35. 5	265. 2
344. 1	574. 1	804. 4	45. 1	275. 3
354. 2	584. 1	814. 1	55. 2	285. 5

295.4	525.2	755.4	985.2	226.2
305.1	535.2	765.2	6.6	236.5
315.2	545.1	775.4	16.1	246.6
325.3	555.4	785.3	26.1	256.4
335.2	565.3	795.3	36.5	266.6
345.2	575.3	805.3	46.5	276.6
355.2	585.4	815.2	56.4	286.1
365.1	595.4	825.3	66.6	296.1
375.4	605.3	835.3	76.3	306.1
385.2	615.5	845.5	86.5	316.5
395.3	625.2	855.3	96.1	326.5
405.3	635.2	865.2	106.6	336.3
415.1	645.5	875.3	116.4	346.3
425.5	655.4	885.4	126.7	356.2
435.1	665.2	895.2	136.2	366.1
445.1	675.1	905.4	146.5	376.1
455.1	685.2	915.1	156.6	386.4
465.1	695.3	925.1	166.4	396.2
475.4	705.2	935.5	176.5	406.4
485.2	715.6	945.3	186.4	416.3
495.3	725.1	955.3	196.4	426.6
505.4	735.4	965.3	206.6	436.6
515.5	745.1	975.6	216.4	446.3

456. 2	686. 6	916. 5	157. 3	387. 4
466. 1	696. 1	926. 3	167. 4	397. 3
476. 1	706. 4	936. 6	177. 4	407. 4
486. 4	716. 2	946. 3	187. 3	417. 4
496. 1	726. 3	956. 6	197. 4	427. 4
506. 2	736. 6	966. 1	207. 3	437. 2
516. 3	746. 4	976. 1	217. 4	447. 2
526. 1	756. 4	986. 3	227. 6	457. 6
536. 1	766. 3	7. 2	237. 2	467. 3
546. 5	776. 1	17. 2	247. 3	477. 6
556. 5	786. 2	27. 4	257. 1	487. 3
566. 1	796. 2	37. 4	267. 6	497. 1
576. 3	806. 3	47. 5	277. 1	507. 3
586. 1	816. 2	57. 1	287. 2	517. 2
596. 5	826. 6	67. 1	297. 3	527. 1
606. 2	836. 2	77. 3	307. 2	537. 1
616. 5	846. 6	87. 5	317. 5	547. 3
626. 5	856. 4	97. 2	327. 2	557. 4
636. 2	866. 6	107. 5	337. 1	567. 4
646. 5	876. 2	117. 1	347. 2	577. 1
656. 5	886. 2	127. 4	357. 3	587. 1
666. 6	896. 6	137. 5	367. 2	597. 2
676. 5	906. 3	147. 3	377. 1	607. 2

617. 6	847. 5	88. 2	318. 5	548. 7
627. 4	857. 4	98. 1	328. 3	558. 3
637. 1	867. 1	108. 2	338. 4	568. 3
647. 1	877. 5	118. 6	348. 4	578. 3
657. 4	887. 4	128. 3	358. 2	588. 6
667. 1	897. 5	138. 4	368. 3	598. 2
677. 1	907. 3	148. 2	378. 5	608. 2
687. 6	917. 1	158. 1	388. 4	618. 2
697. 4	927. 2	168. 4	398. 4	628. 4
707. 2	937. 5	178. 6	408. 6	638. 4
717. 3	947. 3	188. 4	418. 5	648. 5
727. 4	957. 6	198. 1	428. 6	658. 3
737. 3	967. 3	208. 7	438. 1	668. 2
747. 4	977. 4	218. 5	448. 5	678. 3
757. 1	987. 5	228. 4	458. 1	688. 6
767. 1	8. 5	238. 6	468. 3	698. 4
777. 2	18. 2	248. 3	478. 2	708. 1
787. 4	28. 2	258. 2	488. 1	718. 4
797. 6	38. 2	268. 2	498. 5	728. 1
807. 2	48. 1	278. 2	508. 4	738. 2
817. 2	58. 1	288. 2	518. 5	748. 1
827. 4	68. 4	298. 5	528. 1	758. 3
837. 2	78. 2	308. 4	538. 3	768. 5

778. 1	29. 1	259. 1	489. 3	719. 3
788. 4	39. 3	269. 3	499. 2	729. 2
798. 4	49. 2	279. 5	509. 5	739. 3
808. 3	59. 3	289. 4	519. 1	749. 1
818. 4	69. 3	299. 6	529. 2	759. 2
828. 5	79. 1	309. 3	539. 1	769. 4
838. 3	89. 5	319. 5	549. 2	779. 4
848. 1	99. 4	329. 2	559. 3	789. 1
858. 5	109. 2	339. 5	569. 3	799. 1
868. 6	119. 3	349. 1	579. 4	809. 6
878. 3	129. 3	359. 5	589. 2	819. 1
888. 3	139. 3	369. 5	599. 5	829. 3
898. 2	149. 4	379. 2	609. 3	839. 4
908. 4	159. 6	389. 6	619. 2	849. 2
918. 6	169. 2	399. 2	629. 4	859. 4
928. 2	179. 1	409. 4	639. 2	869. 3
938. 2	189. 1	419. 3	649. 6	879. 6
948. 6	199. 3	429. 2	659. 3	889. 3
958. 5	209. 4	439. 3	669. 5	899. 2
968. 6	219. 3	449. 4	679. 4	909. 4
978. 5	229. 3	459. 5	689. 1	919. 5
9. 3	239. 4	469. 1	699. 1	929. 2
19. 2	249. 3	479. 3	709. 3	939. 3

949. 4	180. 6	390. 4	600. 5	810. 4
959. 1	190. 7	400. 1	610. 4	820. 1
969. 1	200. 1	410. 3	620. 6	830. 2
979. 4	210. 1	420. 1	630. 1	840. 6
10. 3	220. 3	430. 4	640. 2	850. 6
20. 1	230. 4	440. 3	650. 5	860. 5
30. 5	240. 1	450. 6	660. 5	870. 5
40. 2	250. 5	460. 2	670. 3	880. 4
50. 6	260. 3	470. 6	680. 7	890. 3
60. 4	270. 4	480. 6	690. 2	900. 6
70. 4	280. 1	490. 5	700. 5	910. 5
80. 3	290. 5	500. 3	710. 2	920. 4
90. 6	300. 6	510. 2	720. 6	930. 3
100. 1	310. 1	520. 6	730. 6	940. 2
110. 6	320. 2	530. 5	740. 6	950. 6
120. 5	330. 1	540. 1	750. 7	960. 1
130. 4	340. 5	550. 6	760. 6	970. 2
140. 5	350. 5	560. 3	770. 4	980. 5
150. 4	360. 4	570. 3	780. 6	
160. 6	370. 3	580. 6	790. 4	
170. 2	380. 3	590. 3	800. 4	

If you liked this book, you'll love this series:

• Little Giant Book of Optical Illusions • Little Giant Book of "True" Ghost Stories • Little Giant Book of Whodunits • Little Giant Encyclopedia of Baseball Quizzes • Little Giant Encyclopedia of Card & Magic Tricks • Little Giant Encyclopedia of Card Games • Little Giant Encyclopedia of Card Games Gift Set • Little Giant Encyclopedia of Dream Symbols • Little Giant Encyclopedia of Fortune Telling • Little Giant Encyclopedia of Gambling Games • Little Giant Encyclopedia of Games for One or Two • Little Giant Encyclopedia of Magic • Little Giant Encyclopedia of Mazes • Little Giant Encyclopedia of Palmistry • Little Giant Encyclopedia of Puzzles • Little Giant Encyclopedia of Superstitions • Little Giant Encyclopedia of Toasts & Quotes • Little Giant Encyclopedia of Travel & Holiday Games • Little Giant Encyclopedia of Word Puzzles • Little Giant Encyclopedia of the Zodiac

Available at fine stores everywhere.